MW00680273

Reader's Reviews from the first Edition of: AM I BRAIN DAMAGED?

I am Lori's Mother and I cannot express the pain and anguish her Father I experienced during her recuperation. In reading "Am I Brain Damaged?" over and over again I have been enlightened. I pray for every parent who deals with a situation as this. If I had this when Lori was in the hospital I would have taken comfort in reading a survivor's perspective on all aspects of brain re-creation and the multiple attempts to return to the world of the non-brain Injured. *That is, after my initial shock, of course.*

Dorothy Jean Purdy, Author's

Mom

Lori's book is a valuable tool to both the patient and those who are caring for the recovering individual. You will see recovery through the eyes of the patient and also get more than a peak at the feelings and emotions that she is experiencing. Don't miss the opportunity to glean from Lori's experience and make your own go a little smoother.

Greta Emling RDH and co-author of: " Wounded Trapped and Voiceless... All things Are Possible"

A TRUE ACCOMPLISHMENT

As a health care professional and a polio survivor with emotional and physical scars, I can appreciate the challenges that the author experienced while overcoming her disabilities. She was able to share openly her feelings, struggles and accomplishments on her road to recovery. What an amazing lady. Thumbs up to Lori and her support system.

Ellen Kaplan, P.T. Michigan

I have worked with many people who have suffered different aches and pains from various car mishaps. Since reading Lori's version of pain and suffering I feel that I have increased compassion for auto related physical malfunctions.

I recommend "Am I Brain Damaged? Return to Life After My Head Injury" to all people including medical personnel as a reference tool with insights from the patient perspective.

Dr. Adam Rodnick, Chiropractor-Rodnick Chiropractic Union Lake, MI

I was very touched by Lori's book. I appreciate the time she took to write her experiences. I think her book is good for the caretakers of a brain-injured person. My 22-year-old son became brain injured two years ago. We are still in the limbo stage. Lori's book not only gave me some insight on what my son may be feeling but also it gave me hope that there is more healing to come. Thank you Lori.

Ms. Hannah R. Anderson

I worked with Lori, at Mc Donald's, when w were in High School, in the late 1970's. I have just reconnected with Lori this year, 2011. I purchased two of her books; one fo a client of mine (insurance) and one for myself. As an insurance representative I speak to people daily on the importance of medical coverage, disability assistance and death benefits. In reading Lori's perspective on rehabilitation and recuperation I have a new understanding o the mental anguish and frustration families could be left with. I suggest "Am I Brain Damaged?" to families of all people who, fo whatever reason, have become disabled an all people in the business of service to others regarding their future .

David Gresehover
Sales Representative Western & Southern Life

In 2009 Lori sent a request to promote "Am I Brain Damaged?" to the Ann Arbor Chapter of the BIA (Brain Injury Association.) I met Lori the day she presented her story. It was not good to hear the pain us survivors share but comforting to know that we are not alone. Some members reported a sense of encouragement. Lori has put her misfortune to good use. Last year Lori worked the BIA booth at the Ann Arbor Art Fair, she distributed association information and sold her books. She donated a portion of those sales to our BIA chapter. The AA BIA chapter looks forward to her next visit and recommends her book presentation to all support groups.

Jim Briggs,
President Brain Injury Association
-Ann Arbor MI, Chapter

am I brain
DAMAGED?

Memoir of Return to Life After My Head Injury

Updated Edition: April **2011**

LORI PURDY FAITEL

Author & Advocate

Community Liaison – North Oakland Chapter
BRAIN INJURY ASSOCIATION OF **AMERICA**

Certified / Licensed
OCCUPATIONAL THERAPY ASSISTANT
C . O . T . A . / L

Traumatic Brain Injury Survivor from 1986

www.**yourbestmadebetter**.com

Am I

Brain Damaged?

Memoir of Return to Life After My Head Injury

Updated version April 2011

All Rights Reserved.

Copyright © 2009: Lori Purdy Faitel

not be reproduced, transmitted, or stored in whole or in part

by any means, including graphic, electronic, or mechanical

without the express written consent of the author/ publisher

except in the case of brief quotations embodied in critical

articles and reviews.

CREATED AND OFFERED IN THE UNITED STATES OF
AMERICA

SPECIFICALLY,

I AM A MICHIGAN RESIDENT

Introduction

At one point during my recovery, I remember telling or being told that I was alive because God wanted me to be. To this day I am sure I was kept alive to serve others and utilize what I have been through to help people. I have used this mantra through the years of recuperation and professionally as an Occupational Therapist.

When something has become hard to handle, or difficult to learn, or perform professionally. . .

I have known God is behind
me, and his plan for me is, to help others.

-Lori Faitel

February 2, 2008

It took years of therapy, determination, faith, and the support of those around me to transform into the woman that I am today. I began this journey as a small caterpillar trapped in the cocoon of rehabilitation. I came out the vibrant butterfly I am today.

"How do I explain something I don't even understand?"

I was in a car accident while driving to work one day. I was registered dead, then in a coma.

My mind grew from that of a preborn child, later re - matured to the adult body I housed, in a matter of 6 years. I have written this book based on memoirs kept from the time I could write again, *I think I was mentally about 4 or 5 years old*, I kept notes for about 20 years.

Completion of the first edition happened after college, *for the second time*, and successful return to the world of the Non-Brain Injured.

I cannot begin to explain what I went through, nor can I give accounts from those I am closest to. My husband, Adam, has requested to never read, hear, or see details about this book.

At this time (2011), Adam is a little more open to discuss the torture he experienced during my
recuperation. When I eventually create an audio of this story, I am certain he will listen.

My parents have both told me how proud and happy they are in who I am today. They also have expressed how the memories of their minutes, hours, days,
months and years continue to haunt them.

As time heals all, my mother has read and reread my story, she tells how she would have valued something as this when I was initially injured and through my recuperation as it would have eased her and perhaps given her insight of the future.

I am basically the same person today that I was prior to the closed head injury. A lot of detailed aspects to my personality, demeanor, and temperament have changed.

For the goodness and compassion I have achieved (in my mental rebirth) I truly love the person I am today.

In the long run, I feel all the changes have enriched the re-creation of my personality.

I like me, and I truly have empathy for others, those traits were not in my character prior to the injury.

I work part time as a Certified Occupational Therapy Assistant/Licensed, I have taken the life devastation of a Traumatic Brain Injury and changed it from a life standstill; into the life enrichment of helping others as I build my future in that of an author.

My email is <u>bisurvivor@yahoo.com</u> and I encourage ideas for distribution, marketing and input from my readers.

In these memoirs you will read the most intimate and private moments in my life.

I have known since the late 1980's that I would eventually have the courage to delve into my written notes. I pray this book opens the eyes of the general public to our lives (referring to my fellow B.I. surviving sisters and brothers), additionally to provide support for the significant people in our lives. The years of recovery changed not only my life, but also that of many people important to me. I see this novel as a very significant piece of art. Allow me to invite you to my private world, share with my happiness, sadness, confusion, my return to normal life and ultimately me of today.

TABLE OF CONTENTS

CHAPTERS

CHAPTER ONE

How It All Happened

I live to enjoy every minute of today, tomorrow may never come.

-Lori Faitel

As with any other workday, my alarm went off at 6:10 am. The life I began, as an up and coming businesswoman, and my excitement with my new independence from my parents came to a devastating halt. On Friday April 25th, 1986, the last day of the workweek, I pushed snooze twice and got up at 6:28 a.m.

Every day I pushed snooze, somehow it made me feel like I was getting bonus sleep time. I always pushed snooze at least once. With each repeat of the alarm, I could quickly look at the time, do the math and determine if I could condense my morning routine, and still make it to work on time. I tried to always be the first person to arrive to my department. I was proud to be known as a prompt employee.

I had recently been promoted to executive secretary, and worked under the Administrative Assistant and the CEO.

The night before, I was in a class until about 10:00 P.M. *I was* taking classes to improve my status in at work.

It was my last class that quarter and I had lived through the final exam. It was a class I didn't like, must have been something related to math.

I was following a plan of study suggested by one of my colleagues at the Western Wayne Oakland County Board of Realtors, a governing board for local Real Estate Professionals. The class was at O.C.C., a local community college, and 15 minutes via the freeway from my apartment.

After the final exam, I stopped at Fibber McGee's, a local pub just across the street from my apartment. A buddy from class and I had one celebratory beer. I emphasize only one beer because I generally did not like beer. When friends asked me to join them for a drink on a work night, I would order a beer to curb any possibility of wanting a second drink.

This was our home. For Robin, my roommate, and I: This

was our first home away from of our parents. Robin was one of my favorite girlfriends. We hadn't met each other until 11th grade, and that was because we had a friend in common who introduced us. Once Rob and I got to know each other, we realized how much alike we were. When I planned to move out, I knew I needed someone to share the bills. Robin was the first person I thought of. I knew that I could live with her.

I can still visualize it. Robin and I had furnished our apartment with old furniture donated to us from friends and our parents. It was a two bed-room on the ground floor. I talked Robin into letting me have the largest bedroom across the hall from the bathroom. My room was just a few steps to the living room, adjoining kitchen space, and front door. This was my private apartment during the mornings. Robin slept in until after I left for work, so the portion of the apartment from my bedroom to the entrance was all mine. I had no family to interrupt my routine and I did not have to live their schedule.

My room was directly across the hall from the bathroom. Getting up and rolling into the shower was an easy task.

I took a shower, blow-dried my hair, and then went back to my bedroom. I looked for the outfit I had put together the evening before. I always did so, to ensure that I didn't wear the same outfit twice in one week. Once dressed, I made my bed.

After showering, dressing, and making my bed, I moved into the kitchen area. I had a 9-inch black and white Zenith on the table. As I became comfortable in this first home of my own, I enjoyed using the kitchen table as a make-up area. Since high school, I had listened to the morning news while I dressed for school. Now, in my own home, I found I could watch TV at my own kitchen table. My morning companion was "Good Morning America."

As I heard Gibson's voice, I put a mug of water in the microwave. When I heard the *ding*, I knew the water was hot. Daily, I looked in my cupboard to choose the flavor that motivated me, of international coffee. I sat down to watch T.V., load up on caffeine, and put my make-up on. That day, the news was mainly about the Chernobyl nuclear reactor accident in the Soviet Union.

At the time of the broadcast, I only caught a few words here and there. I thought this was just another story of Imelda Marcos and her shoes. As I did the initial editing for my first edition of this story, I brought this to my mother's attention. We were both amazed that such a world disaster had taken place and neither of us acknowledged the significance until 2008.The other major story was about Joan Collins and a future interview about her new book, "Joan Collins Superstar". While I was making my bed, I was startled by the sound of the phone. A call in the morning was unusual for a weekday. I had a phone in my bedroom; also we had an extension in the living room.

I grabbed my bedroom extension as quick as I could so as not too bother Robin's sleep. It was Robin's boss. Since she worked past 2:00 A.M. at the pizzeria the night before, I hated to bother her in the mornings. Robin asked me never to wake her until noon, when we first moved in together. So...I gave it one shot by lightly tapping on her bedroom door, she didn't

wake up. I took a message. I finished making my bed and got
dressed. I put on a brand new pantsuit, in my favorite color
pink, that I had received via Newport News the day before.

Because of my new promotion, I tried to dress the part
everyday. I wanted to always look professional. To continue
professionalism into my private life and since this was my first
apartment, I wanted my room to look neat and clean. I left the
door to my room open when I left for work. I knew Robin had
visitors during the day and I wanted them to see by a glimpse
into my room how I was a neat and organized professional.

I performed my regular morning ritual of makeup; I looked
at my eyebrows-did they need a pluck?

Curled my eyelashes, and applied mascara.

**I have always loved jewelry and each time I purchased a new
piece of clothing I also purchased an inexpensive or costume necklace
and earrings to match. I hung my jewels on the wall above a mirrored
vanity table in my bedroom. I purchased this vanity when I was a
child at a garage sale from one of my parent's neighbors.**

With my jewelry displayed in that manner, I could start to
decide which accessory would be perfect for the day's outfit
as soon as I got up. I loved to accent my clothing, and still do.
Instead of going to my closet to choose which shoes I would

wear, as many other women do, I looked through my matching jewels. That day, I decided on a contrasting ensemble to enhance the monochromatic pink of my pantsuit. My final touches were always to stop back in the bathroom where my curling brush would be warmed up. I could then strategically place a few curls in my baby fine hair, and hopefully give it a little fullness & fluff. Tons of hairspray and I was ready to go.

It was a very sunny day, truly the beginning of spring. I had a short walk up two or three steps, through a cement first floor hall, and down some steps to the parking lot where our mailboxes were kept. Because my apartment was on the ground floor, I closed and locked the door to ensure Robin's safety. Then, I walked the usual path to the sidewalk and through the landscape to the large community parking lot. My apartment building was one of six in the complex. Mine sat far back, away from the main road. I entered my car and lit a Marlboro Light.

Oh, I can't believe I used to enjoy the taste and the relaxation smoking gave me.

I had smoked from the time I was a young teenager until my recuperation.

This car, a silver two-door Toyota Corolla, was my first. I always had a car to drive since I had begun driver's training. My dad, Ed, passed his old cars on to me, provided I kept them up with regular oil changes, kept them clean, and was responsible for any mechanical problems. I remember Dad tried to get me involved in my car maintenance, I did not have to do the maintenance for the engine; but when it was time for something like an oil change, my dad would do the job. I was required to be in the garage to watch and/or assist Dad.

Always, if a cost were way out of my reach,

Dad would make a deal with me and help out financially.

The first car my dad gave me, I named "Matilda." It was a 15-year-old, scratched-up, blue Impala. I had always driven the girls in high school to McDonald's in Matilda on lunch break because I was the only girl with a big enough car. The Toyota was the first car in my name only. I loved my Toyota very much. I took advantage of every free minute in my car to

My first home away from my parents.

Above: **My future husband and I, about 4 months before my injury.**

Below: **This is Adam and I, the year we met — 1982.**

keep it neat and clean, and tried to keep it looking like a professional woman's car. That car was especially important to me because my boyfriend, Adam, helped me find it. I purchased my Toyota a few months before moving into my apartment; Adam had searched in Auto Trader and other used car magazines.

Adam had fun looking at different cars. He made appointments for us to test-drive them. Ever since that first car purchase, Adam has played a huge part in any car purchase I have made. Shopping for my cars with Adam has always been mutually exciting.

I was on the road at 7:45. The building I worked in was about a 15-minute drive from my apartment. The traffic was heavier, as it had been for a few weeks, due to construction of the extension of I-275 toward Northville. The route I drove seemed the same as every other day that week . . . until I reached the freeway. Once I was on the straightaway, I scanned traffic to see where I could merge; I noticed a bale of hay in the road. My options were limited. The freeway was very busy, due to a shift in morning traffic pattern.

I knew I had to change lanes. I checked the lane to my left and saw a white four-door car. Since I was in my small Toyota, seeing a four-door car gave me the impression that I would not be able to switch lanes quickly.

My last memory on the road that day was thinking that I should change lanes. Without even a few seconds to allow me to register disaster was about to strike, **IT** happened!!!!

I never had a moment of, "Oh my God." I never saw the collision. To my right, was a patch of grass covered with construction, materials and cement trucks I had nowhere to go! That is the end of my memory. Later a police officer rescued me from my car using the **Jaws of Life**.

My mom, Jean, said the police were alerted to the accident from a news helicopter reporting the traffic for the day. When I began healing, I bumped into many acquaintances that had heard reports of the accident. People told me of their concern for the driver of the accident, which changed to concern for **my** life when they later learned the report was about someone they knew.

I was rushed from the ambulance to emergency at Providence Hospital in Southfield, Michigan. The hospital was about 20 miles from the accident site. I was, and still am, unable to tell what actually happened and how the collision occurred. The details I know are from reports of witnesses and my parents. The only description of the accident came from an eyewitness who was a truck driver. In my mind, he was the typical truck driver seen on TV, with a baseball cap and chewing tobacco, the driver of a 16-wheeler. I am sure the witness was one of the many trucks I passed each morning on that freeway.

I refused to read the documented testimony, I was afraid.

What I remember from the document, the driver described the pink outfit I had worn for the first time that day. When my parents received the documents, my reading ability was null. They kept a copy of that document for my review when I could read. My parents gave me this document when I was back at my apartment. My reading had improved but was still poor. I could not understand more than a few written words at a time.

I kept those documents and attempted to digest the information many times. As my reading became stronger, over the next 10 years, I read and re-read that document. I tried to build the accident into my memory. I was desperate to add this ingredient to my memory. It still is nowhere in my mind.

The eyewitness must have been in close proximity to me to see what I had been wearing. The driver recounted that a truck in front of me had dropped a bale of hay." She gained on the truck." That must have been the moment that I had recognized my need to change lanes. Before I could make a move, another bale fell on my car. This last bale dropped on my windshield. I spun off the road. Before the drop of the second bale of hay, my memory stopped.

My psychologist, Dr. Ianni, said that my mind shut off. If I had been aware of the impending disaster, I would have suffered a heart attack. Another witness saw my car hit a cement abutment on the side of the road. I was told my car rolled three times. I sued the construction company who owned the truck carrying the hay.

As soon as I was healthy enough to leave the hospital for short periods of time, I begged Adam to take me to the area on the freeway where the accident happened. I begged for Adam to duplicate the route, praying the sight would help with my memory. When I saw the accident site I saw fresh tire tracks and up-turned grass in the location where I had rolled. That drive did not help, no memory returned!

Later, while staying at my parent's home, I was given pictures of my car after it had been hauled to the dump. In those pictures, I easily recognized my car.

The driver's side had been completely flattened. The passenger's side was smashed from the roof to the middle of the door. I thought the car in the pictures resembled a Delorean.

I liked the style of the Delorean, it had a futuristic look. The sides from the doors to the roof seemed to take on a triangle shape, the same shape of my car in the photos.

I kept those pictures in the drawers of my dresser. In continued hope for a memory, I used the pictures in hopes something would come back to my mind.

I took those pictures to the hospital, I showed the nurses. I

showed other patients who rode the transportation van with me. I showed patients sitting in the patient lounge. I showed everyone I could. Showing the pictures helped me because when I tried to use words, I could not express myself.
I remember that my lawyer and my psychologist had asked me to tell them the details from the accident. I tried everything to bring those memories to surface. I was certain that if I were to remember the accident, a cure to my mind would follow.

To cure my brain injury had to be the reason professionals kept asking me to tell every detail I could remember.

I had a memory of a truck in a lane on the freeway in front of me. I had a memory, which I later realized was a self-created image, of an enclosed truck. The pull down door holding the contents inside was open with several swaying hay bales.

As I told my psychologist, I remembered that I had seen a bale of hay fall and land in front of me on the highway. I seriously don't know if I actually did see that or if it was a self-created image. When I finished telling my psychologist of these thoughts, he said the truck involved in the accident was a stake truck, which is not enclosed, but holds its cargo with ropes and poles.

My doctor said that I must have subconsciously created this memory in response to the vacancy in my mind about the experience.

I was told many different views of the accident. The owners of a hair salon I had once worked for said that they had been driving to their shop from home when they saw the traffic and the emergency vehicles. They had been deeply concerned for the poor person involved in the wreck.

The receptionist, Lorri, at the Realty Board became suspicious as time went by and I hadn't clocked in. Eventually, she went to the yellow pages and called local hospitals in an effort to find me.

My mother tells of the most disturbing telephone call in her life. "On the morning of April of 86, I was sitting at our kitchen table working on bills. It was a beautiful, sunny day and I was still thinking about how happy Lori had been when she stopped over to see me the previous afternoon, so pretty in her new pink outfit. Then the phone rang with the worst kind of news any parent can hear. It was a call from the hospital. It was made even more difficult because I had my voice box removed and speaks with an artificial device that sounded robotic. The person calling me would not give me information other than that Lori had been in an accident. She said she could not give any information to a 'machine'. I made it very clear that I was NOT a machine and that she HAD to give me the information. She said the accident was serious enough that I should get to the hospital as soon as possible. At this point, my legs went to rubber and I could barely breathe. The next thing I remember is calling Lori's dad to tell him the news. After calling a neighbor so she would be able to watch for our son when he arrived from school, Ed and I drove to the hospital. Everything from that point was like living in a nightmare. We were taken to emergency and met by doctors who informed us that Lori might not make it and if she did she would most likely be in a vegetative state. The only thing that helped me after that was meeting with the policeman who had been first at the accident scene and informed us that Lori had literally "died" twice on the way to the hospital. I felt that if she had already had two miracles, we could hope for another. My words to any parent who finds them in this horrific situation, is to never give up hope no matter what the doctors say, and I believe that doctors owe it to the family members to give at least **some** hope." -*Jean*, My Mom

Mom says the person on the other end of the phone, from the hospital, thought she was a computer, the speaking device sounds monotone and as an uncaring voice. The caller would only tell my mom to call the hospital regarding Lori Purdy. My mom immediately called my dad at his office and told him of the frightening call she had just received. My father then took over. He contacted the hospital and was told I had been rushed to Emergency and was in ICU. Dad rushed home to pick up my mother. I am certain Mom was beside herself. I am amazed she had the strength to contact my Dad. Dad drove her to the hospital.

No doubt that his mind was very pre-occupied with thoughts of his oldest steering toward death. They both rushed into the hospital. In their rush to my side, they could not immediately find me.

After determining my location in the hospital, they had to wait in the ICU for the prediction if I would live or not. Mom says the wait felt like hours.

"I found out about the accident when your job called to see why you didn't come in. I told that you had left for work already. I know that on the morning news that they said there was an accident I don't remember how I found out about your accident. I don't know if someone called me on it

or that I found out myself through your work. I
believed that I called your work and they told me
there. I had to work at Romano's in the morning. I
had to cater a party of 40. I just remember that I
was crying the whole time I was working, making
pizzas. Everyone wanted to know what was wrong.
I told them that my friend, my roommate, was in a
serious car accident. After work, I came to see you
in the hospital at Providence. I didn't know what to
expect when I seen you. You were out of it and
your head was very swollen. And you were hooked
up with tubes. Your mom was there and we cried
together." *--Robin, my roommate.*

Adam refuses to bring the memories of the accident to
consciousness. John, a good friend of ours recalled, "When I
heard of the accident, I took Adam to the bar". John knew
Adam had a very hard time expressing his feelings. John
thought a drink would comfort Adam. John hoped a drink
would allow Adam to accept friendship and support.

Lorri, the receptionist at work, was most likely the second person in my life to find out about the accident. Lorri and I had been friends since we were 16-years-old. She had always been the friend of mine who kept everyone on top of important issues. She called every friend we had in common, including Robin.

My brother told me that my head was huge. I can laugh today, I directly remember my brother as a young boy telling me, "Your head looked like a pencil eraser." Whatever that meant.

Adam remembered, "You had more tubes connected to you than anything I had ever seen before."

My mom says my head was bruised, my eyes black and blue. My Dad tells how the bones were visible because the brake or gas pedal had ripped through the skin at the top of my right Foot; the cuts were large and deep.

I can still feel chills, *when I stop to think about it*, that I had experienced for a few years after my hospitalization if I walked into any kind of medical facility. The sound of life support machines rang deeply into my soul. Those sounds made me dizzy and unsure of my footing on the ground.

Once Lorri found the hospital I was in, coworkers visited throughout the day. I imagine that the CEO gave them all paid time off to visit me.

"We were all standing in the hall at the hospital, looking around nervously to find something that had to do with you. I saw a gurney being pushed. A sheet covered the person being moved but her feet were sticking out. I took one look at the freshly painted pink toes and I knew it was you. I yelled to everyone: There is Lori!"

-Chris, my friend at work

My parents seemed more vulnerable than my friend's parents. They originated from the rural suburbs of Lansing, maybe a smaller town had something to do with it. I am their first child. I was an only child for 11 years. Dad's sister introduced my parents to each other: Judy, who worked with Mom.

Our family moved to Metro-Detroit in the late 1960's. Mom and Dad still lived in the house where I grew up at the time of the accident. I am sure, as the time passed, and my parents tried to comfort each other, they discussed all the happy, sad, loving, and angry times in my life.

CHAPTER TWO

How Does It Feel To Be
In a
Coma?

Today, people ask, "What was it like to wake up from a coma?" I wish it were that easy, just waking up. I don't know if a coma could be experienced the same for any two people. In my opinion, everyone experiencing a coma lives something different. I don't really know what happened to me. Family and friends tell me that, in the early times of my coma, they watched me stir with micro-movements as people spoke or touched me. People didn't understand but my movements were the results of my subconscious. Documentaries and medical writing state that those of us experiencing a coma have the ability to receive sound and physical touch.

Two of the people whom I had spent time with shortly before the accident, came to visit and later told me of what they experienced. One was an acquaintance from work. Marty was the head of data input. I had worked under her when I first began at the Realty Board. Our friendship continued after

I was promoted out of her department.

Regarding her last visit to the hospital, Marty said, "When I hugged you, your heart monitor became louder and your heart began beating faster".

Marty and I had been in some kind of an argument the day before my accident, it seems natural to me that my subconscious was responding to my previous thoughts of Marty.

Another visitor, Greg, had been like a brother to me since I was 7 years old. "You didn't open your eyes or respond, but when I held your hand you squeezed my hand back."

I remember Greg telling me this story of his visit with a confused look on his face. Squeezing Greg's hand seemed like an act in response to the comfort I would have felt in his presence. Since my family moved from Detroit to Farmington when I was in first grade, I had loved him as a brother. It made sense to me that, when he came to visit and held my hand, the only response I could illicit would be to squeeze his hand in return.

Years later, when I visited my grandma on the day she died, she was in a county nursing home near my aunts, uncles, and cousins in Lansing. Grandma had been in a medication-induced coma. I remember hugging her and kissing her. I slid into bed beside her and talked to her for an hour or so. I nestled my head on her chest, wrapped my hands around both of her hands, and intertwined our fingers. I told her, "We are going to say the prayer our lord gave to us." As I began to pray "Our Father Who Art in Heaven," I stopped to take in a breath. At the same moment, I felt a loving warmth all over my body as grandma squeezed my hands. She continued to squeeze my hands throughout the entire prayer. When I was done, she repeatedly and rapidly squeezed my hands many times as if to say, "Thank you."

Grandma Purdy and I had a very close bond for many years. I lived about an hour from Grandma, so I took a personal day off work every other week over a period of 10 years to visit her. During the time I was visiting Grandma, I was an Assistant Minister and a COTA, Certified Occupational Therapy Assistant. I used to take communion to Grandma and we prayed together. For us to pray together so close to her death was a blessing to me. Just as grandma squeezing my hand makes sense, my squeezing Greg's hand makes sense to me.

A week after my initial admission to the hospital, I was transferred to a long-term hospital room. I had graduated from ICU to a room that I shared with another patient. I needed intense therapy and nursing care until July 1986.

Either at the end of my term in ICU or in the beginning of my term in a normal hospital room, I tried to comfort everyone during a tornado warning. The sirens or the storm did not bother me. Of course, I was very confused. I think my attempt to comfort others at the hospital during the drill was my misunderstanding of what was happening. All the patients were out of their rooms and away from the windows. Today, I can picture how the families of patients and the patients themselves scurried around. Hospital beds, IV poles, nurses, patients and families lined the halls.

All the hospital rooms were emptied of people in preparation for a possible tornado. I think Mom was so impressed with my calmness during the storm. Mom always gave me the benefit of the doubt. She didn't understand that I was confused and I didn't understand the other people and their panic. All I knew was minute-to- minute and the immediate surrounding area. I saw people crying and upset. I have always been a social person. If I only knew of the insanity happening around me, I would try to calm everyone down. I was not being a special person and caring about others, I was bothered by the situation.

My first true memories began when I started to attend therapy sessions in the therapy department, in my Psychologist and Speech Therapist's offices.

My very first memory of therapy is still vivid in my mind. I remember therapists smiling at me while I felt like I was at a carnival. The therapists lifted me up and put me on a huge rubber ball. I remember laughing loudly as though I was playing like a child on a playground. I remember therapists talking to me as I tried to follow their directions. I remember hearing people talk to me, but for a long time I could only think back at people. I couldn't speak the words. I could only think at people.

I don't remember specific directions from the therapists such as instructions on how to walk or crawl, but I do remember the therapists laughing with me as I cracked up at myself. I was encouraged to play like a child and that seemed hilarious to me.

One crazy activity I remember was trying to lie belly down centered over a ball while falling from one side to the other. Those memories are as if I was a child again, I was free to play, fall down, laugh, and cry. If I said I was sleepy, the therapists would put a blanket on a mat for me to take a nap.

It felt like kindergarten all over again.

I had Occupational Therapy-O.T., Physical Therapy-P.T., Speech Pathology-Speech, and Psychological Therapy; soon after my admission to the hospital. Mom says I would tell people I went to rehab at the hospital to "go to my T's".

I never had any kind of therapy before the accident, and suddenly I had this therapy and that therapy, they became my "T's". Therapy extended into outpatient therapy or Day Rehab, after October. Dates for Therapy and Rehabilitation are non-existent to me. My parents tell that they have a poor sense of time and are unable to tell dates. **I have no sense of time**. Both Mom and Dad were overwhelmed by the injury and the possibility that their oldest child's future might be that of a handicapped person. I have tried to remember and organize my memories by sequence. My memories seem to be ordered by the impact I felt. I do remember the change of seasons as my abilities improved, but nothing more. I used all the mental and physical strength I could muster for therapy and to heal. If I played and enjoyed therapy, the time sped by. Most of my recuperation time dragged. Every minute of every day was devastating. I had to work very hard for every microsecond. I had very few happy times.

I remember Donna, my P.T., telling me she had just come from a meeting. At the meeting Donna said she recommended for me to graduate from therapy. She distinctly said, "You will be out before Halloween." As I see it, P.T. was not bedside therapy in my hospital room, but in the therapy department. I remember seeing people my age and younger than me with the ability to move and speak in ways I could not.

By the time I began treatment in the Therapy department, I was leaving the hospital on weekends and going to my parent's home. When I was out of the hospital and a part of regular life, I began to see people living normal lives. People were shopping, going to the library; they saw movies at the theatre, not just on the VCR. Normal people ate meals at restaurants outside of the hospital and drove cars.

When I was alone, I cried for long periods of time without stopping and constantly had severe headaches. I felt hopeless. I had fun in therapy when people were working with me, but when therapy was over the pain and sadness would return. When I wasn't in therapy, people did not help me as I was helped and cared for in therapy.

Donna understood my feelings. She was about my age. To me, Donna was a friend. She was also my teacher. This was a two-sided relationship for me. I felt a sisterhood with Donna, yet I respected her because she was my P.T. and teacher. Donna was the only person I liked and the only person who I thought could understand my injury and me. She was the only person I wanted to confide in.

Donna struggled to find something I was interested in that involved physical movement. She tried to encourage me to do different activities that I had engaged in as I was growing up. I played hopscotch outside, jogged, and played basketball using what she could put together in the Therapy Department. My basketball court seemed to be a children's ball and a wastebasket.

I had never been a very physical person. Every summer before the injury, I attempted to water ski with Adam. I took racquetball classes and aerobics after work at the local community college, but was never devoted to any sport. I told Donna that I had taken karate when I was in eighth grade. I had also taken fencing, tennis, and played softball when I was a teenager. I had not been good at any of them, but as a teenager I had the ability and desire to try. For therapy, I was supposed to try physical activity, even though I knew my body would not work properly.

I had to put the fact that I was an adult out of my mind and try everything again as if I were a child. When Donna saw that I was discouraged to try physical challenges, she met with another Physical Therapist in her department who was active with the sport of karate. I was sure he was some level of black belt. I think Donna convinced him to work with me, because I had told her that I thought he was cute, Donna was always doing things to make me happy. I couldn't do many of the karate moves, but it made my therapy interesting.

I began feeling negative about life. I was aware of my physical age along with my mental and physical inabilities, which made me feel very disabled. I worked harder and harder every day just to gain enough balance to sit up or stand. All I was concerned about was my ability to do simple, stupid things; that everyone else could do while other people my age were making families and supporting them.

I began getting tired of working so hard every minute of every day for simple movements. My friends and family told me over and over again how lucky I was to be alive. This was not luck it was pain! I had no purpose in life. My purpose was only to labor every second of every day to perhaps enable me to maybe have the ability to do simple things, unimportant things.

I asked Donna, "Why am I alive". Donna must have not responded with an answer I appreciated, because I asked this of everyone and I only remember a few answers, the answers that meant something to me, and my mental age.

Once I realized that the purpose of P.T. was to help me regain physical ability, I was more positive. I tried to tell Donna of activities that frustrated me or of acts I knew I had done before the injury but was unable. When I was standing, I needed to hold on to some-thing. I decided that I should be able to put my underwear on while standing, without holding anything. I talked to Donna about many different sorts of activities. She said that we would work those specific activities.

To learn to put my pants on without sitting down, I thought I would have to remove my pants. Donna found a way to work on this task keeping therapy private; we went into a backroom while I tried taking off my pants. For years after my injury, I still needed balance and held to the wall, a chair, or sat down when I changed my underwear. I was determined that one day I would have the ability to get dressed without sitting. I guess a normal person sits while changing underclothes. But I wanted to stand. Five years after the injury, I documented triumphantly, "I can put my underwear on without sitting or holding anything!"

Hahahahahahaha…honestly almost 25 years after the TBI I take pride in standing while I change my clothes, but I am in a hurry I do sit down ☺

I wouldn't stop trying to increase in ability until what used to be the simplest of tasks was mastered. As the tasks became more intricate, my focus of their importance decreased.

Physical tasks normal people did not do daily just didn't seem as important to me anymore. I didn't see any importance in my ability to stand on one foot, since the people I saw in normal everyday life did not stand on one foot. I didn't need to stretch to reach something 8 feet in the air as I was asked to do in therapy, because normal people used a stick or some-thing to reach. When I was asked to practice things people did not do every day, I would get mad and want to concentrate on what I saw as important. I wanted to be able to do what normal people do.

PSYCHOLOGY

As a functionally and mentally healthy adult, I look back at Psychology as the most important therapy.

My doctor directed with different avenues to achieve what was important to me. Contrary to what I know some people think of psychology, my Doc, Dr. Ianni, never told me how act, think or speak.

I had every test possible. Tests in which my doctor would say "The boy walked down the street and…" Then, I would need to finish story. I would immediately think of bad things. If I created a story with a bad ending, I thought Dr. Ianni would think I had a mental problem. I would tell Dr. Ianni the question was dumb and hope he would drop the question.

The only endings for the sentences were: The boy walked down the street … and a car hit him or he tripped and he fell.

Dr. Ianni asked me to finish the story in any way, even if I thought the story was dumb. When Dr. Ianni was asking me questions, I was sure he was testing me to determine if I should be put in an asylum. Every time the doctor asked me a question or for an interpretation,

I tried to ensure my answer would not result in institutionalization. I was afraid to answer honestly for fear of what might happen to me if I answered wrong. When I was a teenager, my girlfriends and I tried to stay away from mental hospitals. We used to listen to and talk about crazy stories of mentally retarded people and mentally ill people who lived in asylums and mental hospitals. I knew of three mental facilities not far from where I lived when I was at my parent's home.

What if Dr. Ianni had the authority to decide my destiny? Wasn't that the way tests and psychology were depicted in movies? I learned to use forethought because of my fear. Every question I answered for Dr. Ianni, I tried to answer as I though a mentally healthy person would, and not say the first thought in my mind. I know I was supposed to answer with my first impression.

Almost daily in therapy, Dr. Ianni asked me, "What did you dream?" I did not remember having a dream for a year after the injury. The doctor told me that I would not get better until I started to dream. I did not dream, but I wanted to be better so I fabricated dreams. I didn't want to be sent to an asylum so I lied and made up dream stories. The best way I could stop the questioning was to say that I had dirty dreams, about men and my dreams were too private to share. Either Dr. Ianni figured out I was making things up. Or has he documented that subconsciously all I think about is sex.

The first time I remembered a dream, I was so excited. I don't remember what it was, but it was vivid and simple. I tried to remember all prior questions from Dr. Ianni. I wanted to tell the doctor everything at our next meeting, but once I concentrated on my dream, I decided not to tell him. My dreams were just simple uncomplicated dreams about things like flowers and boats. I didn't want to waste any of my valuable healing time. The dreams of beautiful, pretty colored flowers and boats were elementary and fun, like the cartoons on kid's shows like Captain Kangaroo. I thought Dr. Ianni wanted to hear about my dreams to straighten out bad thoughts, not the happy and colorful thoughts.

I did eventually begin having dreams, dreams that someone my age probably would have. I was happy that at least my dreams started to have actual characters in them and scenes that seemed like reality not just boats and flowers. When I told of my dreams, as with everything else I told Dr. Ianni, I tried to monitor how much I revealed. After what seemed like months, I finally had confidence that the doctor was not testing me to see if I should live in an institution. I began to think the doctor was on my side and finally told him of my dreams, even when I knew my dreams were not normal. Dr. Ianni told me that, little by little, I would remember my past-both the immediate past and the long term past. The doctor didn't promise I would remember everything, but I would definitely have new memories.

Recently, this has been so neat! Moments in my life that were erased by the injury hate started to become real and come to surface in my mind. I am remembering minutes and days of my past. I enjoy these memories and am glad they are returning. This is magical. The best way I can explain the new memories would be as if today, right now, I were to visit a store from my past, and see candy in a wrapper exactly as it looked when I was a child. Seeing the candy and the exact wrapper would be very familiar and pleasing, but that memory would not surface unless I went to that old-time store. When a smell, sight, or a sound brings out a lost memory, I am amazed. The memories are vivid and believable. The memories seem new, but feel as though I have known them all along. The memories were in my mind, but I didn't know to look for them. I don't know what memories will surface or at what time. When a lost memory surfaces; I embrace it and enjoy that moment. Some-times, a memory will come to me that was lost. It is almost like finding old negatives from pictures taken a long time ago, then to develop those pictures to create a new collage. A collage of pictures from something in past history, everyone had forgotten. I'm ready. I want to remember the accident. I think I could handle it, I think I could view the entire crash. I keep vacillating; maybe I should just put my faith in God. If I truly could handle this memory, it will return.

I continue to wonder about the accident. As I wrote early on I have put in God's hands. If the memory is needed, I am sure it will come back. The most significant change in this attitude is the sense of comfort I have and the complete trust in the Lord's judgment.

Towards the end of one of my therapy sessions, Dr. Ianni read the results of a test I had taken and told me how poorly I had performed on them when I had first taken them. He did this to show me the improvements he had seen. I asked him if, as a student, he also took these tests in school. He said that he did take the tests.

What I really wanted to know was: Who decides what's right on these tests, and since that was his profession, was he perfect? Would he know the correct responses without seeing the answer first?

When I was searching for the reason why God had let me live, I asked Dr. Ianni the same question that I asked everyone, "Why am I alive?"

Sometimes, when I asked this question, I went on to say that I was never going to amount to anything important. I would never be a teacher, or parent, not any kind of boss for a company, and I definitely would never be president of the U.S. So, my life was meaningless.

After several years, I chose to stop working with Dr. Ianni, because some outside influences and what I thought to be personal pride gave me the idea that psychology was for other/different people and not me. I called Doc when I wanted to return to college for O.T. He told me to come back and begin therapy with him again. If he could, he would help me.

I was curious of my ability to study and learn text.

SPEECH

When I was an inpatient and into outpatient therapy I remember thinking speech to be the only therapy that cold help me return to who I was. The only place I felt like the adult my body was. My SLP, Speech Language Pathologist, Claudia always seemed to treat me more like an adult than any other person in my life.

I remember Speech with pleasant thoughts.

Therapy sessions consisted of things similar to elementary school and English class. I did a lot of things similarly to what I had seen on "Mr. Roger's Neighborhood" or "Sesame Street." I learned synonyms and antonyms. I began to tell my friends and family that I ways studying my "nyms", maybe because the first time I had finished school, I really didn't understand what an antonym or homonym was. I enjoyed saying "nyms."

I was happy to relearn vocabulary. I wanted to get re-acquainted with every aspect of the English language. If I learned to speak and talk using proper words, my life would get better. Every session seemed to make sense to me. Claudia knew the language I spoke: The Language of the Brain Injured. If I made an error in describing a picture, Claudia would not just correct me, she would teach me what I did wrong. I always felt Speech was beneficial toward my personal goal to become a normal person. I wanted to learn more than I had known prior to the injury. With Speech Therapy, I could become even more intelligent than I was. Once I began outpatient treatment and was living at my parent's house, I would watch game shows as a study tool. Game shows helped me with the quizzes I had in Speech Therapy. Towards the end of my tenure with Speech, it was the only therapy I appreciated. In all the other therapies, I played games, practiced getting dressed, and was asked personal questions. In Speech, I was treated like an adult. If I played games in Speech sessions, I played adult games. Claudia even let me work on a computer. I remembered that I had worked on a computer back when I had a job prior to the injury.

Once I healed enough to move back into my apartment and begin my days in what I saw as the real world, I no longer wanted to live. Claudia gave me one of the few answers I liked, "You just do not know yet. But you have a purpose". Maybe because I respected Claudia, her simple answer

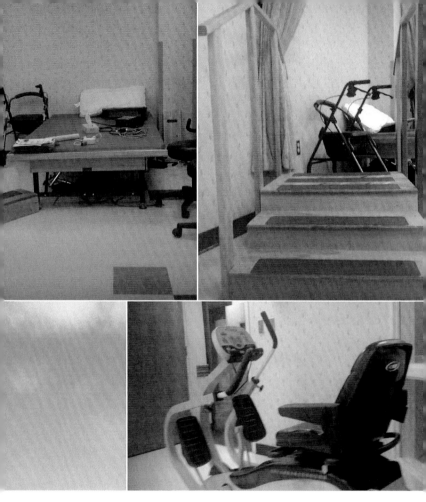

Therapy exercises I became very familiar with when I was an inpatient.

My therapy colleagues and I.

O.T.; P.T.; Speech Language Pathology and Therapy Technicians.

satisfied me.

OCCUPATIONAL THERAPY

**I literally hated O.T! And yes, I am an Occupational Therapy
Assistant. People that know of my life always ask why I chose O.T.
First I was told Speech, which I loved, was a Master's Degree and I
was not even sure I could make a college degree work. Second, I was
told I was not strong enough and that too much math was involved in
P.T. Third, I knew if I became an O.T. I could give my patients a
compassionate treatment and perhaps help them in ways I was not.**

I began therapy with an OTR named Barb. Early on in
O.T., I hated it. I have always been a private person. In no
way did I want to practice removing my clothes, using the
toilet with a stranger; or putting away little toys.

I know I was a very mean and spiteful girl in all therapies.
Later, when I became an outpatient and began seeing things in
a normal state of mind, I sent flowers to the different therapy
departments as an apology.

Barb was my therapist during the most hateful and angry
time of recuperation. I don't remember one thing she taught
me. I bet I didn't have a lot of O.T. back then. Barb worked
with me at my bedside and mostly for

"Activities of Daily Living" or ADLs: bathing, toileting and hygiene. I went into rages when anyone except for my mom tried to bathe me or help me get dressed. My mother took over for all my ADLs, and stayed at the hospital with me 8-10 hours a day. When I was healthy enough to come to the therapy department, Barb was gone. I only remember attending O.T., and being treated by many different O.T's.

Since I have become a C.O.T.A, I have taken classes from and have seen some of the O.T's that filled for Barb when I was a patient at Providence hospital.

One of the first days of my second year of the C.O.T.A program, I was the Occupational Therapy Club President. I went into the Occupational Therapy instructor's office to arrange a time to visit each class and talk about the O.T. Club.

"Excuse me."   A new instructor looked me in eye. Something about her eyes told me that she had once been kind to me. "I'm Lori Faitel."

"I'm sorry, I'm not familiar with the name," she responded "Where did you work as a practioner?"

"Providence."

"What year?" I put one-and-one together. "You must have been one of the fill in therapists when I was a patient at Providence, my name then was Lori Purdy."

She remembered me. We smiled, laughed and spoke for a few minutes about how unusual it was that I would eventually after recuperation go to school to be a therapist.

After my graduation from O.T., Cheryl said she knew Barb, my original O.T in the hospital. Cheryl told me that Barb had brain cancer when I was her patient and she had left the hospital. That is why I had several different therapists. Cheryl contacted Barb and told her of my graduation from the C.O.T.A. program. During the graduation dinner in college, Cheryl came to my table and told me she had spoken to Barb, who expressed her pride for my recuperation and me. She was happy for me, and the direction my life was taking.

There was a place where all of us patients with similar problems ate lunch and meet between therapies, I called it homeroom. In this room, all of the patients for rehabilitation were about the age of my grandparents, with the exception of one other girl and me.

I don't remember actually starting rehab. One day I was there. Early in my remembrances of rehab, vans picked us patients up at our homes. We would then all meet in "homeroom". One girl, another patient, was close to my age. We rode the same van to and from our homes and the hospital. This girl had a similar head injury, but I was the lucky one. She had broken some part of her body on top of having a head injury. Her accident was earlier in the same year as mine. So I knew everything I saw her go through wasn't far behind for me.

One day in the morning, the other girl my age was crying in the day rehab room, not just tears, but sobbing. She said her sadness was because she remembered her accident. This girl said that the psychologist had hypnotized her so she would remember. From that point on in the van, she would jump when she saw a car and say, "It was like that".

I was scared to death. There was no way I wanted to be so scared and shook up. I begged every-one, "Help me. I don't want to remember." Then, I talked to my psychologist. Because the other patient was involved in a collision and mine was not a collision, my doctor said I would not gain anything from remembering. There was no need to hypnotize me. I guess it was good for the other girl to remember her accident, maybe she learned something.

I haven't spoken to her since we recuperated. I wish her everything good. I felt a sisterhood with her. I know what a truly lucky person I am. There is nothing strongly wrong with her, but she graduated from therapy with lasting problems that she will never overcome.

I had asked Donna why the other girl was able to go home. I knew she had worse problems than I. The response, as I remember it, was something about how that girl was recognized to have reached her potential for returning to normalcy. That girl's normalcy was different than the normalcy I was trying to reach. Maybe she was able to accept where her recuperation had taken her. Maybe she did not desire a higher level of functioning. Maybe she was unaware of a higher level of functioning. Maybe she just accepted the level she had gotten to and gave up. Who knows? The decision was made to stop.

Those of us in homeroom had a weekly scheduled time for our therapies; some of us had therapy at the same time. We all had different combinations of O.T., P.T, Speech and Psychology therapy. Our day rehab schedules were individual. Similar to high school, where some classes are shared and some classes were not taken by every student. We had hours or minutes in between therapies. The hospital kept the homeroom open for us all day.

I was told the injury to my brain was similar to that of a series of strokes. I remember homeroom was a large room that reminded me of the lunchroom in high school. Often, we had snacks and our various medications delivered to us by nurses. Therapists picked us up from homeroom and took us to our therapy sessions. Some patients were independent enough to walk to and locate therapy without accompaniment. I didn't understand the layout of the hospital and I couldn't tell time. I needed someone to guide me to therapy and to tell me when to get ready.

As I saw it, people in Day Rehab were not physically and/or mentally able to be independent. Some of the older people I attended therapies with had graduated from Day Rehab and still had memory and loss of physical abilities. I know that the damage to each of our brains was different. In my opinion, due to the older people's ages, they didn't have the motivation.

Because of their personal opinions of life and their ages, they achieved everything they wanted to work for or had the patience to achieve.

As I progressed in Rehab, I tried to help the other patients. I needed to make use of what I was recently able to do. I became close with the two nurses who delivered our medication and snacks. I told them that I knew their job so well that I could come back and work side-by-side with them instead of as their patient.   Maybe this is one of the first times I recognized my desire to work in therapy.

I saw the two main nurses for day rehab daily: Betty and Clara. The position of working with the day rehab patients seemed satisfying. When I was able to tell time and recognize blocks of time I had available, I began to ask other day rehab patients where they had to go and what time their appointments were scheduled. I began, on my own initiative, to determine who needed to go where and at what time. I became a volunteer to transport day rehab patients. I remember Carla, my favorite nurse, who also brought our medications to homeroom, saw what I was doing. She smiled and brought my progress to my therapist's attention.

One time, while I wheeled an older man to physical therapy, he looked up at me angrily. "This is so dumb. I can't do this. I just want to go home." I bent down to this man so I could talk nose to nose with him. I told him that when I came to the hospital, I was in a coma. I couldn't walk and was in a wheelchair until I re-learned to walk without falling. I had learned to balance. I told him it pissed me off playing those games too, but I was pushing him that day.

He quieted down and said, "Oh." Then I said, "Just do every stupid thing they tell you, it works!" I don't know what my encouragement did, if he started to try or not, but what I said was true.

I was once in the same place as the people I volunteered to transport. But, I had recuperated enough to be a wheelchair chauffeur.

Another person, who I wheeled to PT & OT, asked why I continued to re-quire therapy when I was able to wheel them to their sessions. That person had seen me in PT. It seemed to the other patient as though I was practicing ballet at the parallel bars. I don't remember what words I used, but I do remember the instance. I remember laughing to myself and how proud I was of the recognition of my accomplishments from bystanders. I told the other patient that I was wheeling, where I had begun and where I wanted to end up after therapy. As silly as it may have looked, the dancing, the karate and the basketball activities were all a huge improvement for me. I became forward and excited to tell everyone who didn't know about the therapy I had and how it all worked.

I guess the way I remember my recuperation today, is similar to the way in which I remembered my life prior to the injury. While I was recuperating, I could vaguely remember my life style prior to the injury. I vaguely remember my life during rehab.

If I wanted to turn the channel on TV, I could remember

somehow I was able to switch the channels. I may have remembered looking at the television knowing that TV viewers had a choice of several different shows to watch but I did not know how to obtain the choices. I didn't remember that a TV guide was available. I didn't remember a device could be used to see the different shows as they are playing, I had no idea, I knew other stations were available and that I did not have to watch one channel all the time. I didn't remember about a remote.

While grocery shopping after Adam and I were married, I noticed a lady I recognized. I tried to shop close to this lady to get a better look at her. Once I was certain of who she was, I rolled my cart close to her. I wanted to do a victory dance and show her how recuperated I was. I caught her eye. "Is your name Carla?" First, her eyes asked, "Who are you?" Then, she responded, "Yes." "I am Lori Purdy from rehab at Providence Hospital, weren't you my favorite nurse, Carla?" "I would have never recognized you." She looked at me with the warmness she always had in Day Rehab. We had a quick, friendly conversation and went about our shopping. That was one of the many instances where I was able to demonstrate to someone who only knew me as brain injured; how I had finally gotten better. In my mind, encounters like this one are incredible.

Today, when I meet a new person the usual response is, "You had a brain injury?" My happy response is "And you had no idea, did you!"

CHAPTER THREE

Return to My Parent's Home

Let's see . . . as I told earlier, I don't remember dates but I do remember the change of seasons. Today as I look back I seem to only remember the fall and summers. I am very confused if I spent one or two springs at my parent's home, two falls or even a winter. These are pieces I do remember:

While I was recuperating, I had more of a sense of remembrance of my life prior to the injury. I vaguely remember my recuperation. I do not remember the day I moved out of the hospital. I do not remember anything about my belongings, and the shipment of them from the hospital to my parent's home. I do not remember visiting my parent's home on weekends prior to my discharge. I do not remember my first day of life as a discharged patient.

About 9 months after the accident, I was released from the hospital and returned to the care of my parents. Moving out of the hospital was monumental. Leaving the hospital meant I was closer to becoming a normal person. It was my first move from ICU to a hospital room that signified the end of the coma. My move from the hospital to my parent's home signified the possibility of my return to a life in the world of normal people.

My doctors, nurses, therapists and family all agreed that, based on the speed I had healed thus far, I was a good candidate to continue therapy and develop further in both my mental and physical abilities.

Because of that good prognosis, all of the medical professionals who worked with me recommended that I continue with therapy on an outpatient basis once I returned home.

My parents must have become burdened with their new responsibility. I required 24-hour care. I had only improved enough that I didn't need immediate professional medical help. Mom and Dad decided they were up to the task of taking over the care I could not perform for myself. I am sure this decision made them fearful that they may have to live the rest of their lives caring for their permanently disabled adult daughter. I can't even imagine how my parents had to change their lifestyle.

My mom had some experience living with disabilities. She had her larynx removed due to cancer 2 years prior to my injury. For the remainder of her life, Mom needed an artificial device to speak. I was, and still am proud of how she has been able to adapt quickly and deal with changes to all aspects of her life. Mom's internal power structure has been incredible. She was able to take on my injury and continue both our lives as normally as possible, and with a positive attitude.

As with all of the memories I have from my childhood, my parents were always big on celebrating advancement in my brother and my life. With that thought, I am sure my parents made a big deal out of my move from the hospital to their home. I remember the celebrations for my brother as he grew up. Today, after complete recuperation, I can visualize what that day might have been like, similar to how a mom throws a baby's first Birthday party. In thinking of this promotion, from that of an inpatient to an outpatient, I would love for that memory to return.

I am sure the minutest part of my pre-injury brain was aware of the happenings to my physical self. The encouragement my parent's displayed at my promotion from the hospital was equally as discouraging for me, since I had to revert to the home I had lived in since I was a child and not back to my apartment.

I knew that house like the back of my hand. In this case, the return to my parent's home was more familiar to me than my own hand. The rooms were in the same place, the furniture was the same, the entrance and exits were the same, but my hands were not. My hands could not perform tasks as they had always done, at least for the years I lived in that house.

The house was in Farmington, a colonial with three bedrooms upstairs. It was the 6th house on the 6th street off the main road. My old pink bedroom was painted brown and nabbed by my brother, Chris, as soon as I moved out. Chris is eleven years younger than me. My second bedroom at my parent's house had been the guest room, until my parents had to care for their adult daughter all over again. Mom and Dad transformed the guest room into an adult room with what looked to me like a giant baby bed.

I am sure Mom tried to make this room as cheery as possible, but there just was no cheer. My bedroom was at the end of the hall. To get to the bathroom, I would need to pass my brother and parent's bedrooms. Every day, I traveled down thirteen steps to the living room, which attached to the kitchen. I could see through to the kitchen and into the family room, which my parents had built as an add-on when I was still in high school. From the kitchen, I would pass a half bath on the way to the stairs leading to the basement or straight ahead into the garage. The garage opened up facing north and beyond the driveway was a creek.

I remember many times pulling a car out of the garage, I had to make a hard turn right and follow the curve in the driveway, then straight over the side-walk and boulevard to the street. When I was in high school, the aluminum siding at the car entrance to the garage had scrapes on it. The scrapes were from backing out. The rear bumper on the passenger side of a car was the culprit. I knew I had white on my bumper, but I couldn't have been the only person to make those marks. My dad must have turned a little too tightly a few times. Every time we cleaned up the scratches on the aluminum, they came back.

When I took the stairs to the basement again, I counted down 13 steps. At the foot of the stairs, I would turn left and walk into a TV area with a wet bar. Beyond the wet bar was an arch, through the arch a left turn would take me to a steam sauna- shower combination, which was under the stairway.

When we moved into that house when I was 7 years old, I used to meet my dad in the basement at the wall opposite the sauna. This wall separated the pantry and the TV room. My Dad had a wood working table, tools, and a woodworking chair. That was his man cave. Our back yard was visible from the kitchen window and out the door wall that was in the living room. Immediately out the door wall to the back yard was a cement porch and a large backyard. The backyard was fenced with a privacy fence. Just be- yond the fence was a running creek. I remember Chris, as he grew up and learned to walk, he was allowed to play in the backyard by himself.

The relationship between my Dad and I was the exact opposite of the relationship between my Mom and I. I began my life as Daddy's girl. As I grew to a teenager, I decided my Dad was only a man. In my teens, I began a short term of feminism. I respected Dad, but we were not friends. When I was a child, Mom was always around, but I preferred to have fun with Dad. Mom was just a mom to me, until I was a teen-ager. Her job was to cook, clean my room, and launder my 61 clothes. As I became a lady, I grew to appreciate my Mom. By the time I graduated high school, I realized my mom and I had a lot in common and the differences between us were small.

When I think of Chris, he aged from childhood to his late teen years instantly. The gap in my memory of the early years of Chris' life must have been during the years of my recuperation. Chris says he does not remember me, or my recuperation. From 1986-1989, I remember nothing about Chris at all. From 1989-1993, my only memory is when he and my buddy Bill lit the candles in my wedding. I have recently talked to Chris about this and he agrees that he and I both must have been in denial of those years.

By the time Chris was in high school, Ed was an executive. Ed was the primary income earner for our family. As his job status increased, so did the family's economic status. Chris went through different stages of maturity and I infrequently remembered the same stages in my own natural maturity. I remember Chris playing instruments, getting nice new bicycles, new clothes, and was allowed to have many cool pets. I was not able to take instruments in school because of the family budget. My first bike was beautiful; my dad, to be candy apple red with any bells and whistles I wanted, customized it. My parents found them at a discount. I always had nice clothes. I always wanted a pet snake, but my parents would not allow it. Chris had the benefit of me softening my parents, which let him fulfill his desires for a pet snake. Chris had a good fashion sense that must also come from me! I describe my love for Chris as true appreciation for our differences. At the same time, I get chills of happiness when I recognize aspects of me in my brother.

Because of my inability to move about freely, I could not do anything for myself. My parents put me safely on the couch or in a comfy chair where they could see me at all times. While Mom tried to do her regular household chores, she positioned me to watch TV or gave me safe and easy to toys to see, touch, to play with. I had many toys given to me by friends and family. As only a mother can do, Mom helped me with my bath and toileting. I don't remember anyone ever helping me in the bathroom except for her. The entire hygiene situation and my need for assistance in that area made me mad. Thank God, my memory has kept most of my unpleasant thoughts buried.

Similar to a baby's bath seat, Mom came up with an idea. She placed a lawn chair in the bathtub as a type of support to allow me to experience an at home bath and shower instead of a sponge bath. I have no idea how I know this, I remember seeing the lawn chair, but not using it in that manner.

My parents were directed to purchase a hospital bed with sidebars that slid up and down. While I was in bed, the bars were locked in the up position and I was restrained with a soft cloth jacket complete with fasteners to tie me to the bed rails.

I did not have the ability to climb the stairs. I bumped up and down each step. I sat on my butt and pushed myself up the steps backwards. I remembered using that technique when I was a child. The bump technique, which I used to conquer the stairs, enabled me freedom. Dad and Mom were confident in my safety and allowed me freedom throughout the house as long as I only bumped up and down the steps. Every time I went up or down, I counted the steps: one, two, three, four and so on up to thirteen. Each step I climbed was a triumph.

Day to day memories began once I moved back into my parent's house. It was summertime. I don't know what I was

10

64

doing at the time, maybe just enjoyment of the outside.
I appreciated the sensation of grass on my feet for what felt
like the first time ever. One day, I heard the gate to the yard
jingle. I turned my focus to the sound and a dear old friend
was smiling at me. Yeah! It was my buddy Bill who relocated
to Las Vegas a few years earlier. I remember the smile on his
face. I remember my parents greeting Bill and the happy look
on their faces when he arrived. I am sure my parents saw
improvement in my mental strength at my immediate
recognition Bill.

Ed and Jean were about 45 years old when the injury
happened to me. Back then, Ed was an Executive Engineer for
AM General. Ed began working for AM General when I was 5
years old. He started on the ground floor with no experience.
When I was a child, Ed and Jean were struggling to make ends
meet. I was born almost to the second of 9 months after Ed
and Jean's wedding.

Ed was the baby of the family with two older sisters. His
father left the family when he was young and later died of a
heart attack. Ed's mother, my grandma P, lived to be 89 years
old and became my best friend.

Jean was a stay at home mother, and one of the most supportive mothers I have ever heard of. Jean was the oldest in her family with one brother and one sister; both of her parents were very attentive and loving. Jean's Dad, my only grandpa, died of cancer when I was 10 years old, before the birth of my brother. Jean's mom, my Grandma W, also died of cancer in her 60's.

Chris was my baby doll. I dressed, fed and played with him every minute I had a chance. All of my friends in high school loved him. I am sure some friends came to visit me only to play with my baby brother.

When Chris was 13 years old, my life was abruptly halted. He says he doesn't remember much from my history surrounding the accident. His memory begins when I reached normal status again.

I brought Chris to my apartment to watch movies and hang out once a week. I feel I missed a lot of Chris' life. My recuperation took about 6 years. By then, he was 19. Today, as adults, Chris and I openly enjoy and love each other. Life just gets in the way and limits our time together.

Above: **My brother, Christopher, near the time of my injury.**
Below: **My parents – Jean and Ed.**

Above: **My sister-in-law, Marie, I prayed for her to come**
my brother's life for years and my niece, Aryanna
Below: **My nephew, Izak.**

CHAPTER FOUR

When I Started

to Understand

Obviously I had difficulty understanding. For the longest time I did NOT understand anything. As my brain re-developed, I somehow knew bits and pieces of adult life. I looked to others as if I was an adult, but for few years I was mentally a child in an adult body. I do not have the ability to explain in a manner for the non-brain injured mind to visualize. So let me try to explain in basic terms.

I realize that I am very lucky. The type of treatment I went through and the therapies I had were very new. I am very grateful. One therapy is needed that I did not have: "Friend of the victim therapy." I made this up, but I know if the people close to me took a therapy like that, my recuperation would have been better for them and me. Friends and relatives tried so hard, but they could not understand me. I pray that reading my thoughts and feelings can open the minds of friends and family members of the head injured. Perhaps reading this writing will help the non-injured to have more compassion for the injured.

Since I was a teenager, I used the steam sauna in my

parent's home. I referred to the sauna in my parent's house as a spa. I took advantage of the spa once a week. I loved lounging in this area. Back then, I gave myself facial treatments and conditioned my hair weekly.

After the injury and when I had reached a level of comprehension and physical ability to shower alone, I used my parent's spa as I did earlier in my life. As I physically and mentally grew up, I became happy to take showers on my own.

Then, one day as I was showering, I was shocked! I saw human feces on the floor. I was the only person in the shower. I understood that it must have come from me. I went wild. I was so mad that I didn't remember the physical act of pooping. I didn't even remember my body feeling the need to poop. I tried to clean it up. I must have made noises; I heard my mother walk down the stairs, she opened the shower door and saw what had happened. I was so embarrassed. I screamed and cried while my mother cleaned it up. Can you imagine being 25 years old and shitting in the shower?

Mom always cleaned up my messes patiently, which just made me angrier. She didn't mind cleaning, because I was sick. I extensively worked every minute of every day not to be mentally sick. Mom's patience with my inability made my blood boil. If my mom could accept and handle the disgusting messes I created, she must have accepted I had reached the end of my recuperation. Maybe I should accept it also. Maybe I was not "normal". Maybe I would forever be unable to be an independent woman again.

I cried harder, stomped my feet, and ground my teeth together until I felt pain. I will not be mentally sick...No...I won't accept that!

I was still going to therapy as an outpatient. I wasn't finished with recuperation. I was beginning to get re-orientated to life! My disabilities were not permanent, or so I prayed.

Each age of learning, either from birth to 24 years of age or from the injury to normalcy, I wanted to be independent. As I became stronger both mentally and physically, I became increasingly more able to function without help. I wished, as my function increased, others would also accept that I was developing. I was in a return to a normal life. I wanted everyone to think I was FINE! I was starting to do normal things.

I began to move my body in ways a normal person my age would. I ate normally. I walked slowly, but normally. I used the bathroom alone. I was physically independent. However, I could not remember beyond a few minutes. I was far from mentally normal.

My therapists and family were happy with my ability to talk, express ideas, and see the world around me. I was not satisfied. My improvements were only accurate minute-by-minute. What I saw as happiness in others made me mad because I hadn't learned to repeat an action correctly. I wanted to do it correctly every time!

Adam took me out as often as he could. I was like a child who could walk around safely, but was not aware of other people. I didn't understand that I needed to act appropriate in society and the dangers of trusting strangers. Adam took me to the mall where I was happy to look at pretty jewelry and clothes, eat lunch, or visit a candy shop. For me, the mall was a playground. I had no agenda. I had no purpose in life.

Once I was able to differentiate and understand options were available to me, I understood that I could make choices. I appreciated weekends. As I understood, I had freedom to spend my days with whom I wanted and where I wanted. I was not limited on the weekends, by the requirement to be in therapy at a certain time each day or only able to eat at certain times. I was gaining independence. When each day of the week was the same and each meal was purely nutrition, I didn't care about different days or different meals. Until I knew I had choices, every day and every minute was the same.

I saw nothing to look forward to. Making choices and the ability to have choices made a huge difference in the strength of my memory. As I had lived in society prior to and after the injury, I realized that to live life in the manner I wanted, I needed the freedom to come and go as I pleased.

I had to take a form of drivers training at the hospital. To begin driving on the road again legally, I had to retake the driver's test at the Secretary of State. Since my return to normal life, I have repeatedly become frustrated at senior citizens and the general public. I wish all people with reduced with reduced mental functioning were required to take driver's training.

I want to take this opportunity to ask all drivers reading my memoir remember that a car can be a weapon and the life of the driver is only one of many things to consider. Every car on every road is a large and very heavy piece of equipment. If a driver has any decreased ability, I pray for the driver to find a safe route of transportation via public transportation.

As a defense mechanism, I would tighten my fists and grit my teeth when I was unable to anticipate or problem solve. I desperately wanted to look normal to onlookers. Until this point, I didn't realize I had the power to correct errors. I didn't even recognize errors. My response to a loss of understanding or mental ability was outbursts, stomping, and slamming of my hands into the table.

Each time I was given a new and more difficult task, I was excited. I understood, as people spoke in adult language and my rehab seemed to concentrate on my life rather than my ability to move, I was getting closer to normal.   As I began to walk and move more regularly, I developed aches and pains in my neck, shoulders, and back. I told Donna about the new pain. She then began an ultrasound treatment to heal the pain and instructed me to begin exercising at home on my own. For many months after I moved out of the hospital, I began each day with floor exercises. I thought of my body from my head to my toes as I exercised. I performed every movement that I was taught in therapy.

Donna suggested I get wrist weights when I was still an inpatient. Of course, my parents bought them immediately. As soon as I brought my new weights to therapy, Donna created an exercise program for me to work on at home. I also wore the wrist weights throughout the day at my parent's home to help strengthen my arms. My old raggedy wrist weights became a friend of mine. I will probably keep them forever. I think they are the only remnant from my sessions.

My parents have tried so hard to help me understand my feelings. Of course, no one can understand the kinds of feelings I had. To help my parents see things from my point of view, I explained every detail to them. I told my family to think of themselves on an escalator going down, and the escalator next to them going up. If they blinked as they turned their head quickly to the side, wouldn't they feel a little unsteady? I felt that way every time I tried to walk. I tried not to use escalators.

Another analogy I used was: Let's say you're at a social gathering and you are having a drink. After a little while, someone from across the room calls your name. You turn fast and the room feels like it is just an instant behind you when you turn your head; or how about on a sleepy afternoon? It's cold outside and you just curl up for a nap. You're almost asleep and the phone rings. When you turn your head fast but don't get up, the room seems to be a step behind.

I was afraid I had not healed from the eerie feeling the escalator gave me, when I turned my head, or as I was beginning to stand up, walk, and sit in a chair. I feared that I would regress in my mental capability. Any sudden movement gave me head rush. When I was still healing from the injury, I was unable to distinguish between a head rush and dizziness as an after effect of the injury. As I recuperated and before I returned to normal life, I was always afraid I would regress. The transportation van always waited for me to get into my house safely before it moved on. It was protocol for one of the attendants to walk a patient to their door, but I would not allow them walk me to the door; I wanted to do it myself. One day, when I was dropped off in my driveway and got to my parent's front door, I tried to karate kick it open, but I fell. I got up as fast as I could and waved to indicate that I was ok and deter the van drivers from helping me. I always have and continue to karate kick doors open or kick automatic door openers when my hands are full.

I thought that, if I lived each day like a normal person, I would become a normal person. I asked everyone who knew me prior to the accident to talk to me about who I was. Did I have a temper? Was I a nice person? What was my favorite food? What was my favorite color, perfume, song, and movie? What did I like to do on my free time? Who was I?

If I had enough history and details I could recreate the pre-injury me. I was sure as deeply as I could sense a difference, I would someday morph back to the original me.

Adam took me to a Phil Collins concert, our favorite singer of love songs. One of the most important things about that concert was, when I had to go to the bathroom. The concert was at The Palace of Auburn Hills. The Palace was like all other stadiums with lots of seating, food and beverage stands, and a bathroom for every thousand people. *I am exaggerating.* Adam had confidence in my ability to locate and use the bathroom by myself. I never thought that many of the concertgoers had been drinking and they were oblivious to people around them. If I had recognized the other concert attendees had been drinking, I would have been less inhibited and would not have felt everyone watch me. To me, I had to ensure I could find the bathroom, use it properly, and get back to my seat in what would be considered as a normal amount of time, so Adam wouldn't worry. I needed age appropriate encounters to allow me to have age appropriate responses and communication skills. During my recuperation, I experienced maturing without the benefit of childlike innocence.

I had to experience learning to be a girl, politeness, social ability, problem solving, and how to respond to fear, disappointment, satisfaction and happiness all over again.

My parents, my brother, Adam and I went to the family cottage near Mackinac Island for a weekend in the summer. When we were walking down Main Street on the Island, I told my parents that I was uncomfortable in crowds. I was very familiar with Mackinaw Island I worked on the island for a month or so the summer after my graduation from high school. I knew every inch of the small island, all the tourist attractions and the remote areas.

I tried to visit Mackinac Island yearly from the time I was 19 years old. Every step I took on the island had fun and pleasant memories, but not that year.

Crowds drove me crazy. Crowds don't walk in any definite pattern or at any regular pace. I said they walked in "clouds." The clouds in the sky seem to just float by. Sometimes, a plane flies through them and changes their pattern. Sometimes the clouds look spread out, while other times clouds are tightly bunched up. Clouds seem to have their own private agenda with no regard to anything surrounding them. That is how I saw people when they moved in crowds; as walking in groupings of clouds.

As hard as I tried to become the person I once was, I tried to learn to live life as though a normal person would. When I attempted to move or talk, I was aware that I had done these things prior to the injury. I was an adult with adult thoughts, but I could not express myself like an adult. I did not want anyone to know that I was like a child or someone with mental difficulties.

I was Lori Purdy, the Lori Purdy that back in the spring of 1986, was an independent businesswoman moving up in the world. I was proud of myself. I had worked hard for the first 24 years of my life to become who I was. A car accident left me with a closed head injury, which resulted in the removal of my previous accomplishments, friendships, and social status.

I don't laugh like I used to. I don't talk like I used to. I don't snore, smile, blink, sneeze, cough, clear my throat, comb my hair, take a shower, or brush my teeth like I used to.

After my recuperation, some distinct aspects of my personality changed. I don't smoke any more and feel as though I never did, but I know I used to. My leisure time became more productive. I learned to appreciate every minute that was normal.

I always had many friends. Friendships were always easy for me, until after the injury. I never thought twice about my balance, it was easy for me to walk anywhere. I ran up and down the stairs at work and in my apartment complex. Today I walk more gingerly up and down stairs and I rarely run anywhere.

My belief in God became deeper and my love of the human race has been enhanced since the injury. All of these details and more have recreated my personality.

I am still myself, but better. This time around, in building my personality, I have had the opportunity to painstakingly consider which aspects I want built upon and which aspects I don't like. Many details of the personality I had before the accident has been reworked into aspects I am proud of. I like the Lori I have developed. Unless a person had known me really well both prior to the injury and after my recuperation, they wouldn't know I had changed.

I held on to many aspects of my pre-injury personality. I

thought that, to be accepted again and build new relationships, I had to be the person I was. When I finally let some the old me go, I was at a point where I could say, "I am who I am. And I like me."

After trying to be something I was prior to the injury, I had finally become comfortable with what I called the "new me". People liked the new me for whom I am at today, rather than wanting me to return to the Lori of my past.

I feared being less of a person than I was prior to the injury. I feel blessed and very happy to have emerged as the Lori I am today, I am luckier than most. Before, I liked who I was, but after my recuperation, I like me even better.

CHAPTER FIVE

The Drive

This chapter was the first chapter I worked on with an editor. This tells of the most private times of my recuperation, yet this needs to be heard. Imagine a 25-26 year old woman who had only the thoughts of a pre-teenager. As a person ages, in normal life, she learns what is appropriate; and sometimes what is spoken and done by the opposite sex could be interpreted completely not as originally meant, or taken to literally. Mental maturity allows for unspoken and intelligent reasoning.

Our memories are like a book that is not bound. Place the book in the wind and the top pages will blow away. The top pages are our short-term memories, while the bottom pages are our long-term memories.

Today, I understand the blessing that I survived.

In this chapter I was released from the hospital, I was driven Monday through Friday back to the hospital for outpatient therapy. I have no memory of the beginning of outpatient therapy, I am sure I was still in my wheel chair, that attendants came to my parents home and wheeled me to and from the house and the hospital. For the first time as I write this and look back at my what my level of mental functioning must have been when this began I realize not only that the basis of my actions were wrong. But that the person involved was very wrong to participate.

While with my parents, I was as dependent on them as I was in childhood. My mother helped me with bathing and other daily tasks as I learned to become Lori again.

My drive for independence was strong. I fought every step of the way to break through the physical, emotional, and mental limitations caused by the accident.

Through those years, I was hungry to become "normal" again. Normal was a term I heard over and over again. That word echoed in my head be- fore I could talk, before I could express myself, before I felt like a person again. Even after I began my mentally healthy life, as an Occupational Therapist, I have used the term "normal" describing someone prior to an injury or a person with no unusual physical circumstances.

As I began my recovery, I realized the necessity of reinventing myself. My recovery was long and difficult, but complete. Although I am "normal" now, back then, I felt as though I was in limbo. Portions of my old self remained, yet I hadn't fully developed into the person I am today. Becoming the "New Lori" was a long process in which I had to relearn not only the most basic daily routines like bathing, dressing, and brushing my teeth, but also how to think, feel, behave, and live among other people.

Today I remember minutes of my time at my parents home, as I concentrate on them the minutes sometimes become hours of different activities but I do not remember a complete day of the year or so I spent back with my parents.

The rehab van picked me up at my parent's home and dropped me off at the hospital along with a group of other outpatients. I remember feeling uncomfortable riding in this van to the hospital. Not because of the ride itself, but the fact that it illuminated the reality I wasn't normal yet. I couldn't wait for a time when I could travel back and forth to appointments in a car like a regular person.

Once I had mastered the basics in my therapy sessions, the focus turned toward developing social skills. I began to reach out to new people around me. As I gained confidence in my new self, I expressed my joy and tried to make connections with those around me. "I love you," was a common greeting I offered those around me. I have always delighted in socializing with people and showered loved ones with affection.

Around this time, I began to realize the awakening, or re-awakening of my sexuality. I remember three distinct opportunities to act on my new curiosity and desire. I indulged in only one.

The first of the three opportunities was with Porthos, another rehab patient, who was around my age. He was at a similar stage of recovery, experiencing a similar reawakening. I remember his pride when he confided in me that he could still, "Get it up." I encouraged him to take care of that on his own.

The rehabilitation therapists at the hospital often placed Porthos and I together. Perhaps they hoped that we would connect with one another and have a romantic bond. Although I'm sure that I could have taken advantage of this opportunity for an encounter with him, considering the curiosity of our newly awakened desire, I refrained.

One day, I was walking down the hall in the hospital. I unsteadily held the wall for balance. I glimpsed a face I knew, a nurse, Diana, a friend of mine from high school. She approached me and touched my arm saying "Lori, are you alright, why are you here?"

I admitted that I was actually feeling better than I had been in months. I explained how I was an outpatient and a closed head injury survivor. I shared that I was at the hospital for outpatient rehab.

Diana and I rekindled our previous friendship. That day, I asked her to drive me home.

On the way home, I remember telling her about my new life, how everything was new to me, and how I wanted to start having sex again. I was referring to my boyfriend, Adam, who had been with me since before the accident. I had asked her if I could get pregnant if I resumed having sex at this time. My uncertainty stemmed from the fact that I hadn't had a period for I don't know how long. She told me to protect against pregnancy no matter what the chances were of me getting pregnant. She then told me she used the contraceptive sponge.

Adam and I had been together for approximately 4 years before the accident. He stood by my side through my coma and rehabilitation. When I got home that particular day, I told him about meeting Diana. I explained she was a nurse and that she had told me we could resume having sex and advised me to use protection. I don't know how, because I am sure I couldn't have arranged it, but someone bought me a package of sponges.

The drive to be normal grew in intensity. I yearned to have normal relationships with everyone, yet I couldn't feel normal with Adam. Perhaps he was a reminder of who I used to be and not who I was striving to become. I didn't understand how he could be in love with both the old and new me. It seemed impossible in my mind, I wasn't the woman he had originally fallen in love with.

The association in my mind between him, the accident, and my former life were preventing me from moving forward. I needed to grow beyond my relationship with him. We broke up when I tossed some of his personal items out of my apartment.

Let me reiterate my living arrangements. I went directly from that of an inpatient at the hospital to my parent's home. After about a year of advanced care and advanced therapy I became able to function with "stand by assist" or someone to keep an eye on me. For this reason Robin my roommate back from prior to the car accident

worked with my parents and provided the stand by assist. After about a year of recuperation with my parents I excitedly moved back to my apartment, back to my old bedroom, back to my old closet, back to my the world independent of my parents. I believed I was on my way to the "normal" life that was stolen from me.

Around this time, I began acknowledging D'artagnan, one of the rehab workers at the hospital. I don't know how I did it, but I had asked D'artagnan to take me home. I didn't want to ride home in the rehab van with the other patients. I wanted him to drive me home in his car. He accepted the request and drove me home that day, just the two of us, alone. I didn't even consider if he was married.

Well he was married, I understood the concept but it just wasn't real to me. I felt as though this was my first date. Even as this was happening the days and minutes did not seem real to me. I began playing a part, as if I was a character in a movie. My courage increased as each scene evolved. This was just an episode of my new life. I was acting scenes. I acted out what I thought any woman my age in this situation would do.

I moved in for a kiss. D'artagnan welcomed my affection. I enjoyed being an adult, kissing a stranger, and luring him into my lair. We became intimately involved. I acted the part of the young girl who was blossoming into a beautiful, seductive woman, desired by every man.

The affair was never planned. I consider it an affair because he was married. In my mind, we were actors in romantic scenes not reality. I had no emotional connection to him. I was just acting to become the woman I had imagined. I was acting out uninhibited thoughts.

Things became more serious, at least on his side of the relationship. While I was living out this story, he was becoming more attached. During one week- end rendezvous, he gave me a gift. It was an emerald ring.

In the sparkle of the stone, I suddenly saw myself and snapped into reality. I saw our relation-ship for what it was. This most certainly was not a story. I realized this was actually my future. My eyes, heart, and mind saw everything around me with greater moral clarity. In that moment, I knew what I was doing was wrong. I recognized this relationship as a response to my recovery. I didn't approve of how I was leading my life. My moral compass caught my attention.

I knew I had to end this relationship. That's how I

remember it. In my mind today and deep in my heart, it doesn't seem like that was me who lived that life.

It seems as though the affair was a drama, a play, a movie I had seen. I don't feel a real connection to this experience since I don't feel a full connection with the person who put on this performance. It wasn't the old Lori who did those things and it wasn't the new Lori either. It was a Lori in limbo, the one in the cocoon, soon to emerge in my new form.

God has allowed me to grow past this, yet I don't feel remorse. I don't remember the relationship as my own reality but as a story. I manage to keep it locked away from my reality. Today, I accept and know the person I was during this exploration was not the Lori I am today. That Lori was only alive for a few years. She hurt people emotionally and did bad things. I can't change it now. I have stored those parts of my life away.

The relationship between D'artagnan and my-self was short, but felt like a long time.

He tried to keep in contact with me, and had even told me that he was getting a divorce. I clearly explained to him that I didn't love him and it simply didn't matter to me. I am now married to Adam. He loved me not only before the accident, he loved me during my rehabilitation, and he loves me as I do him.

During the affair, I had wandered down a path that was absolutely wrong for me, for anyone. I am grateful for all the people in my life that helped me and stayed with me during my recuperation. My concern grows for Head Trauma victims and the lack knowledge to help in this area.

CHAPTER SIX

Love and Marriage

1982 was a year of changes for me, I decided my occupational path of cosmetology was not meeting my needs, my mother was diagnosed with and survived cancer surgery and I met my husband.

I began dating Adam in October of 1982, at the time I was seeing a few other men. When we met, I was a 20 year old and a student in his father's Principal's and Practices of Business class at OCC (Oakland Community College in Farmington, Michigan). I met Adam first when I went to my professor's house with my hair cutting experience to make some extra money.

My parents were very agreeable to let me use the upstairs of their house, on the second level was my bedroom and a full bath down the hall, to cut, color and perm hair. I carried my hair scissors with me at all times and I could do a quick cut in the bathroom at OCC, at someone's home or where they worked.

I cut Adam, his dad-John, and his brother-Brian's hair in their home after I was a student of John's. I dated Adam, very casually on my end, for months before I was ready to date him exclusively.

Adam easily became one of my favorite people to hang out with, I remember telling friends as I brought Adam to social functions or had a date with him; that I didn't expect the relationship to develop beyond friendship, I enjoyed his company very much and wanted to be his friend for a long time. As we dated I was completely unguarded in my behavior, unlike most 20-year-old girls when they date. I was not trying to make an impression on Adam, each time we spoke or met I knew in my heart that I was just going to enjoy the time and if my style did not fit his; I would to move on, such as I would with any new friend. Before Adam I had this attitude with only girlfriends.

By the time I moved into my apartment I had made some love life decisions.

I remember, my one time hairdresser, grandma telling me that a woman should be married by the time she is 25 or she won't ever get a chance. I Robin and I moved into our apartment in January of 1986 when I was still 24 but May was coming and I would soon be 25.I guess I made the age of 25 my personal deadline. Adam and I had continued our relationship and it had unexpectedly blossomed into a serious love. One of my most important goals was to become Adam's wife, or in the least to be his fiancé by my 25th.

Adam and I had dated for a number of years and I was tired of the waiting game. My plan to speed up this romance was to tell Adam of a new goal. Adam and I regularly made goals for us and shared our goals with each other. After dating Adam for 4 years my new goal became: By the time I was 25, if I was not engaged to Adam, I would begin dating other men; I was not getting any younger.

Adam will never admit it to me, but I think he and I were in the midst of engagement to be married when my injury happened. I was living in my apartment near 12 Oaks mall. Adam and I frequented the mall for dinner and a movie. On several occasions, we stopped to look at engagement rings in the jewelry store windows .

During recuperation, I misinterpreted everyone who tried to help me. More than any other person, I misinterpreted Adam. When I returned to my apartment Adam came to visit me regularly.

Adam had begun working in Real Estate Investment. He purchased distressed homes, fixed them and rented them out. He began this business when I was in data processing at the

Board. I had access to listings of the homes. Adam built his real estate business into a full time job.

He had an answering machine for different ads he had in the paper; the ads were to find homes to purchase, to talk to other real estate investors and for potential renters to call. When Adam came to my apartment, he would go into my bedroom every few hours, close the door and use my phone.

A thought came to my mind about Adam regularly going into my bedroom, closing the door so I couldn't hear what he was saying, and using my phone. I was sure that he was tired of being stuck with a disabled girlfriend and that he was calling to find a healthy girlfriend to pick up for a date after he left me.

I had my pride. I was not mentally healthy yet, but I tried to be the independent woman I was prior to the injury. Since I decided Adam wanted a healthy girlfriend and wanted to find another, I didn't want him either. After using my phone for what seemed like weeks, but was most likely a day or two, I hit a boiling point. Adam came out of my bedroom after a call and I threw him out of my apartment.

"I hate you Adam!" I pushed him out my apartment door, slammed the door, and went to my bathroom to get his personal items. I grabbed these things and ran out to Adams car. He was sitting in his car when I got to the parking lot.

I walked up to his door and banged on the window. When Adam rolled his window down, I threw his toiletries in the car and told him never to come back.

At that time, I had started to see D'artanyon. He told me that he understood me. He said he loved me, he couldn't leave his wife but he "truly loved me."

I dated Dartanyon for a few months.

Robin tried to hook me up with some male friends of hers. I am sure she was doing her best to guide me to be the marriage respecting person I had always been in the past.

She knew Dartanyon was married.

As time heals all, Adam is slowly able to discuss and participate in discussions regarding this book. Recently at work, at a skilled nursing facility where I am a C.O.T.A., I ran into an old High School friend's mother. That friend I haven't seen for many years and I used to think it was because the friend didn't like the person I had become. I told Adam of seeing the mother of my old friend, whom he also knew. Adam asked "why don't you like her anymore?" I told that as I was recuperating and had interactions with that friend she seemed rude to me. The friend seemed irritated with me and disliked of me. I had

decided within myself that she no longer liked the Lori I had become so I dismissed trying for a reconnection.

Adam looked at me with great concern on his face as he told me he had done the same to me as that friend had and why did I continue our relationship. I told Adam the two relationships were very different and that I recognized his attempts to be with me. I did not recognize any attempts from the friend. Adam then told me he has though out all these years believed he had done me wrong. Adam was retreating into my bedroom at my apartment because he couldn't handle seeing me in my decreased mental and decreased physical state.

I may have misinterpreted everyone's friendship and level of comfort they had with me. If I wasn't a professional therapist today I don't know if I could handle seeing a friend in the state I was in. Adam and I have a wonderful relationship and he is my best friend. If I hurt any of my previous friends before, during or after my brain injury it was unintentional. Friendships are hard to come by, what I treasure in my memory of early relationships is what was good. I pray that all people I was once close with will find the compassion to forgive, move forward and try to forget the unhealthy Lori that I once was.

Adam called me at my apartment at least once a week. In the beginning, I hung up on him. Then, as he kept calling, I began talking to him a few sentences at a time until we re-built our friendship over the phone. When summertime rolled around Adam invited me to come visit his family at their lake cottage, which was about 20 minutes from my apartment.

That invitation reminded me how many years Adam and I spent at the lake before, how I had known his family, his brothers, and parents closely for more than 4 years.

My memory improved, my understanding of daily activities grew. After dating a few man friends of my girlfriends, and never liking any of them, I began to realize my relationship with D'artanyon was immoral. I realized I was living a life that I completely did not agree with

I was seeing Dr. Ianni on an outpatient basis at that time. I spoke of the break up with Adam, but never spoke of the relationship I had with D'artanyon, because they knew of each other. Dr. Ianni helped me remember the feelings on marriage and fidelity I had before the injury. I remembered religious teachings and my previous belief in true love.

I realized I still loved Adam. My thoughts were pretty regular, but I continued to have a difficult time expressing myself verbally. I learned that I could write letters. In letters, I had the ability to erase and change sentences and word structure. In a letter, I could rework the words until they read clearly.

I began writing letters to all of my friends.

I wrote a letter to Adam telling him of my increased ability to think properly, how I realized I had never stopped and that I continued to love him. I knew that Adam had evening classes and his answering machine usually picked up at night.

One evening, I called him with the plan to read my letter to his answering machine. The letter was in my hand as his phone rang. I was ready to read it. On the 4th ring, Adam answered the phone.

I was surprised. "I thought your answering machine would pick up, I wrote you a letter, May I read it to you?"

Adam said, "Please do."

When I finished the letter, Adam was silent. I said, "Did you fall off your chair?" I was afraid of how he might respond.

Adam took a deep breath, "Can I come over?" Within 20 minutes of hanging up with Adam, he was at my apartment door. We hugged and kissed and hugged and kissed. I cried and asked him never to leave me. I remember that night as the beginning of our true love.

I married Adam on November 11, 1989 I am proud to be Adam's wife. I like being his wife. I enjoy the comfort and support of a spouse. I wouldn't cheat on or leave Adam, ever, I mean ever.

We will most likely argue about things to do and places to go. We will change and grow different from each other. We will be grumpy, we will be happy, we will have our own private triumphs and losses, but I want to be Adam's life partner through it all.

When my return to the normal world became certain, Adam asked me to never to review with him any aspect of my recuperation. Adam and I lived together for one year before we were married. I re-member one night Adam shook me awake "Lori, please change your position, you look too much as you did when you were in the hospital".

After Adam and I were married and I was working as a COTA, D'artanyon called. Adam answered the phone "Lori, you have a call." I answered a different extension, "Hello" "Hi, Lori, do you want to get naked and talk to each other" said the familiar voice on the other end. "Don't you ever call me again?" I slammed the telephone down.

I was in shock after this call. I began crying and couldn't stop. Adam put his arm around me and asked what was wrong. "That was D'artanyon who I had an affair with when I was attending outpatient rehab. Adam, he was married and you know I would never do that in my right mind."

Adam held me close told me he understood that I wasn't the real me when the affair happened, God knew I was messed up and all is forgiven.

One day, prior to the only engagement I truly know of, I asked Adam if he was with me because he felt a responsibility for me. Adam told me a story of a situation when he was a teenager: he was dating a girl and she was in a car accident. The girl broke her leg. Adam dated her for longer than he wanted, until his dad told him that he did not owe that girl and if he felt it was time to date other girls, he should move on. With that story, Adam told me he was with me because he wanted to be, not because he felt he had to be.

So many times through my recovery and into today, Adam helped me with his love, comfort and support. I remember so many things I don't think I can write the huge impact that Adam has had on my life.

Adam never told me how to do things. He never shaped my opinions, unlike some of my friends think. To this day, we disagree. But, because of Adam's part in my life, I have learned to handle disagreements quietly. I have learned that I don't need to win an argument. I don't even need to get my opinion across.

If I have a disagreement with anyone or anything, I just look at the situation and decide if I need to act on it. If no action is needed, sometimes I just walk away.

If I must act on a disagreement, such as in work, I try to stop and remove myself from the heat of the disagreement, then revisit the act when I am calm I find it easier to make the proper decision. This technique works so well.

I distinctly remember Adam saying to me, over and over again, "Don't worry, and come back to the problem later." Needless to say, my family is perfect. My kids: 2 cats and 2 dogs, love me unconditionally. My husband loves me for who I am and what I am. I thoroughly enjoy every minute I am a part of.

CHAPTER SEVEN

Outsiders ##!!@##!!!!!!!!********

It seems some people took advantage of the fact that I didn't know things. It seemed some people were intentionally mean to me. Some people took advantage of my loss of memory and tried to build a characteristic into my personality that I did not have prior to the injury. People flavored their descriptions of events to persuade me to make decisions, some of which I may never have made on my own. Maybe people thought a different view or outlook was better than my previous outlook. I am sure people wanted to help me in whatever ways they could, but I know I was told a few cooked-up stories. People realized that I was putting every part of my personality together. I needed guidance as to right and wrong. I learned about legal right and wrong, moral right and wrong, and religious right and wrong. I also learned that almost everyone created his or her own interpretations of what was right or wrong. I did not understand much, but when I would perform an act, I knew in my soul whether or not the act was something I would have done prior to my injury.

By the time I wrote this entry I recognized actions I had previously been a part of that were not what the first Lori would have accepted.

People helped guide me, but they imposed their personal morals upon me. I did not understand good or improper, but I new if the guidance was different from my pre-injury personality or not.

I wanted to die. Death was surely better than the life I was living. I do remember I wanted to stop living. I wanted to leave this earth and go to heaven. I prayed daily and asked the lord to take me.

Approximately one year after the injury, I wrote: I don't believe things can be put off until tomorrow, because there is no promise that tomorrow will come. Because of no promise for a tomorrow, I wrote my own layman type of Will and Testament for all of my personal things. I went through every - thing I owned and documented them, regardless of the value. I put my documentation in a good place, an easy place for people to find it. I checked every once in a while to make sure I remembered the location, and if everything in my possession was included.

I continue to try not to put things off until tomorrow. I'm definitely impulsive. My impulsiveness seems to be because I want to make events immediately a part of me. If I put an event off it, may never be a part of my history. When I think or hear something I would like to do, read, listen to, see, or visit, I want to do that activity ASAP.

I don't mind making plans for the future, but I don't like to wait around. At work, home, and in social situations I am able to wait an appropriate length of time, but privately I am bouncing around inside while I wait for the proper time to come.

When I was at the Board, a friend at work mentioned Atlantic City, sounded fun, I told Adam and we went. There were a lot of things that I to wanted to re-learn or learn for the first time.

I don't remember where I was emotionally when I wrote: I am sure as I think today. I want to do it all. I want to try and experience every enjoyable activity I had heard of.

To learn something new couldn't be that hard. After all, I had learned to walk again. There were not a lot of emotional wants I had. Emotional wants involve other people. The wants

I had were personal, experiences I wanted to become a part of my life, part of my personal history. I only had a limited amount of control as to how to go about getting these experiences.

Like Tim McGraw sings: "Live like you were dying". To have a complete life and my craving for experiences satisfied, I needed to experience everything that seemed enjoyable.

Before the accident, when I had been stuck in traffic for any period of time, I could not sit still. After the injury I lived through many weeks of being confined to the bed or chair because I was unable to walk from place to place. When I was stuck on the couch, I prayed and begged, "Just let me up...I even want to be in a traffic jam".

Once I returned to the normal world, I appreciated traffic jams. They don't bother me anymore. To be honest, I appreciate the extra time to myself. During a traffic jam I am not confined. At least not to a bed, and not somewhere that makes me feel like I am disabled.

When I told my mom of these prayers, she said, "Be careful what you pray for." Yes, I am in a lot of traffic jams and I get cramps and backaches pretty often. I asked for it, but

I almost appreciate them. When I didn't understand, I didn't recognize regular daily aches and pains. I love regular daily aches and pains.

Mankind is more important to me now after the accident. People don't seem to realize how important their minutes are. It makes no sense for someone to spend minutes being upset because a glass has broken, they stubbed their toe, it's raining outside, or some other little insignificant thing. We can get over it and go on.

I spent many hours trying to find something to do when I was only allowed to lie on a couch. I would have loved to stub my toe or get wet walking in the rain.

When I was in Day Rehab and in homeroom I was with many people. Mostly the others in Day Rehab were stroke victims. I was told that a Closed Head Injury requires similar therapy as that of a stroke. My therapists were the same people who specialized in geriatrics.

All of us in homeroom were at various stages of speaking. We all experienced memory loss and specific muscle loss that is needed to communicate. I bet we sounded pretty funny when we sat in one room together. One of my personal ways to re-learn words were to read the dictionary and the thesaurus from beginning to end.

The best way I can describe what was happening to me, is that in my head, I knew what I wanted to say but I couldn't speak the words. Currently, in dealing with peri-menopause, I am losing words sometimes in mid sentence, which is similar but different to my loss of words early on in therapy.

I remember trying to have a conversation with my mentally healthy friends and co-workers, but the language I was able to speak was very limited. As I developed my language skills by listening to others, playing crossword, word searches and reading; my verbal vocabulary grew.

My speech matured to that of normal for a person of my physical age. For a long time after the injury, my temper was short. Was it left over from my pre-injury personality or a result of the injury? As I recuperated, I learned to think before I spoke, which was an improvement. I took the time when something bothered me to think, "Will an outburst help?" Sometimes, I would get angry, but not in the same way I had pre- injury. If I decided I was upset about something trivial, I realized that I would waste my precious time going into a rampage. Time became something of great importance.

Pre-injury, I was loud and short-tempered. One evening after class, my girlfriend and I had just gotten into my car when I put my key in the ignition and realized I had mistakenly left my glasses in class. I screamed, swore, and hit the dashboard for about 5 minutes. Then, I ran into the school and retrieved my glasses. When I came back, my girl-friend told , "I was scared of you."

Maybe, partially due to impulsiveness and partially due to how important every minute is to me now, I consider how I want to spend my precious minutes. I prefer to spend all of my minutes in something that is pleasant. If I become anxious, I try to deal with what bothers me, I don't get mad. I get past sad times and concentrate on pleasant minutes. If I must live unpleasant minutes, I try to minimize them. Since the injury, my temper has not vanished completely.

I went through what my physiologist called rages. I could not communicate with others. Someone could say something as innocent as, "The sky is blue," but I heard it differently in my mind. Regardless of what was said, I heard that person mock me. I thought the person said something negative to me, in a manner I was not familiar with. I tried gentle ways to release my temper. I hit my pillow. I grasped my hands together so tightly that my fists turned purple and would shake. I clenched my teeth, so hard that I thought I had cracked them a few times.

These mild temper tantrums were a controlled type of rage.

I realized how important minutes are and my desire is to be normal. With those techniques how I was in control. I saw my psychologist and often and asked him, "Why am I wasting my time getting so mad at these little things?"

One Sunday afternoon while I was watching TV, I watched a documentary about head injuries. The television show highlighted a man who suffered from a head injury, the rages and temper tantrums he experienced were on video. His wife had made pancakes for breakfast. For no apparent reason, he got mad and threw his plate. After seeing this program, something clicked. I realized how stupid it was for this man to throw his plate. I knew he thought he had a god reason, but he was confused. I realized how much I thought I understood what the man on TV was thinking. I knew why he was mad. My next appointment with my psychologist went well. I told the doctor what I had seen on TV and that I understood that rages are "normal". He then informed me that these rages are a vital part of the healing process. He said that there was a lot of anger in me, which I am told, is anger at the whole accident situation. Doc told me that I had to let this anger out. I was always more comfortable with animals than with people. But after the injury my pets I find the quickest and easiest source of relaxation and happiness to be with my pets.

Currently if I want a pick me up or to take my mind off of the world I go to my favorite PET SMART and spend time in the kitty room. My youngest dog will soon take the exam to be a certified therapy dog. We will both have our certifications ☺

I remember when Adam and I were dating, before the injury. I would visit the house Adam lived in with his dad. At that time, I liked cats, but could take them or leave them. To me they were just another beautiful animal. As we be-came more involved and I spent more time at Adam's home, I became friends with his cat, Sam. Sam had free run of the house inside and out. Sam and I built such a human-cat bond. I could sit in the kitchen and call out for Sam. No matter where he was, inside or out, he would come running to me. This happened between the years of 1982 and 1985 anywhere from one to four years' pre-injury. For me to build a bond with a cat at that time in my life was unusual.

After Adam and I were married and in our first house, John, Adam's dad said Sam wanted to live with us. We had Sam for a few months and I talked Adam into visiting the Humane Society to get another kitty. I loved Sam, but I wanted a kitty. A friend for Sam, the kitty we chose was a grey and black, a Siamese mix he was small enough to curl in Adam's hand. I wanted to give kitty a masculine name. The name I came up with was Hobie. I wanted to find a name that Adam would appreciate, that would not be too feminine, Adam generally thought of cats as pets for girls. Since Adam and I had enjoyed our summers riding a Hobie Cat sailboat, the name for our new kitty, 'Hobie' was perfect! Hobie was great and Adam loved him as much as I did. From that point on I decided I would always have a pet cat.

Chapter Eight
Work Life

I was unaware if I would successfully return to work. Was I able to return to a situation that I was satisfied in? Would I ever be content? I remembered self-respect prior to the accident. I used to have goals, and prior to the injury I was motivated for advancement and development. Would I ever have a passion for life as I did before?

As I said earlier in my story, I had been working for The Board of Realtors when the car accident happened. I was comfortable at the Board and planned to work with them for many years. I was lucky in that I liked everyone at the Board. I spent work and leisure time with them.

Prior to working for the Board, I had been a hairdresser. I worked for a year at a salon, The Mane Connection. Before that, I filled in for my hairdresser friends at the salons where they worked and did hair out of my parent's house. As I came to know co-workers, some of them asked me about my previous job then immediately asked if I would cut their hair. I went to their homes after work. I became familiar with the family and friends of my co-workers. I made additional, fun money, by cutting hair. I honestly and proudly referred to all co-workers at the Board as my friends. My friends spanned all departments: printing, data input, maintenance, accounting, human resources, marketing, the members from individual real estate agencies, and the CEO. The Board of Realtors was a blessing to me as I recuperated. I met Judy, the Administrative Assistant at the Board, when I was taking evening business classes at OCC. At the same time, I was working at The Mane Connection. I was trying to learn a career with more earning potential than that of hairdressing and my skin needed less exposure to chemicals. My hands no longer could suffer the creams, lotions and chemical processes involved with doing hair.Judy played a huge part in my life, from just prior to my employment at the board, all through hospitalization, and into the beginning of my return to the normal world.When I decided to move out of my parent's house, I told my co-workers. The CEO, Dan, gave me a wine decanter and some wine glasses as a house-warming gift. Judy gave me furniture and dishes. My co-workers became like an extension of family and they helped me, each of them in their own special way. I had no experience in using a Laundromat, buying groceries for myself, reception of bills in my name, and the responsibilities that came with life beyond parents. My co-workers, with more life experience, taught me in much the same way a big sister or brother would. Intimate details like: how to find grocery deals, how to create simple easy foods for dinner and lunches, and what life was like in an apartment complex. I had been promoted from data input to the secretary of the CEO and Administrative Assistant in November of 1985. My car accident occurred on the way to work the following April. After hospitalization, I went back to the Board of Realtors. Both Judy and the Dan worked closely with my parents, who then also worked closely with my therapists to create a type of return to work therapy. This therapy, created by my family and co-workers, was more important to me than any I received in the hospital. Judy was my main source of guidance. She ensured that I was given very easy jobs and tasks, such as filing and stuffing envelopes, which later developed into my ability to fill an opening for the receptionist position at the Board. Judy not only helped me at work, but she opened her home to me. She asked me to begin giving her manicures again. Judy & her man friend, Adam & I double dated. I re-learned about life at work and socially through Judy. I began working at the Board an hour or two a day and progressed to a day or two a week,

until I was able to work a 40-hour week. I continued outpatient therapy while I was back at the board. Judy used to review therapy with me and tailored my learning. She told me during review of therapy, how proud she was of me. I was embarrassed that I created toys in therapy. But, because of the support I received from Judy, I was not embarrassed to give her a wooden car I made- all by myself in O.T. Actual job tasks were exciting and made me feel like an adult, not the silly things I did in therapy. Sure, they were simple tasks like stuffing envelopes, filing, alphabetizing, and talking on the phone. I thought I was doing well. The people at work were always nice to me and tried to always be positive. I interpreted the kindness as approval. Judy and other co-workers called and told my family, "When we think Lori has learned a task she suddenly reverts to totally misunderstanding the job."
I was familiar with office products, the blue print of the offices at the board, but not my job or job related tasks. If I encountered a word or situation I had no experience with since the injury I had no idea what to do. My co-workers were wonderful; I just wish they felt comfortable to tell me to my face what I was doing wrong. Looking back today, I can

understand my co-worker's apprehensions. I did not remember how to alphabetize by name, and a name that consisted of two parts, like-Mc Call threw me off guard. I am sure my intermittent difficulties surprised my co-workers. I very much walked normally, spoke normally, did portions of tasks normally and easily.Unexpectedly, an aspect of a task would confuse me. As I learned or remembered tasks, I thought I would be given different degrees of responsibility.

Once I had conquered one type of job, I was eager to move on to more advanced tasks, I wanted my old job back. I thought the Board was going to help me progress, and help me re-learn my previous job position. I never thought of the costs involved and manpower needed to re-educate me. I might never re-gain ability to return to my previous position. It would have taken years to build my knowledge to return to the position of Administrative Secretary. I continued with the Board of Realtors until I became overwhelmed by my anger at the loss of my prior job. Judy said I should have been proud, because the lady who replaced me also came from data input. She used the notes I made when I had the position. It became obvious to me that I would never have the ability to return to the position of Administrative Secretary. I had too much to re-learn. I became afraid that, as I was told prior and during recuperation, I had reached my peak in life. My employment status was to stop at that of a receptionist. I thought about it and felt that for improvement socially, I needed to accept that I had reached my peak in business. I began talking to co-workers and Board members asking if I could keep my position of receptionist and take on another job. I wanted to bring my income up to what it was prior to the injury. Since I was unable to work at a higher paid position. As soon as I let acquaintances at the Board of Realtors know that I was interested in a part time job, a member of the board said he needed a receptionist at his real estate office. I appropriately asked Dan if it would be a conflict of interest for me to accept that extra part-time job. Dan said the part time job would not be a conflict with my receptionist position at the board. Before I even thought of the additional part-time job, I was angry all the time. I was truly mad at myself because I did not have the ability to return to my previous job status. My headaches returned with a vengeance and I easily became angry with Robin and the people I loved. My psychologist suggested my anger and pain could be alleviated when I allowed my anger out. After work each day, Dr. Ianni said, I could vent my anger. I would be alone and no one would see or hear my tantrums. Once some of this anger was allowed out, it would be easier for me to manage my life. When I began the part-time job at the real estate office, I was beginning to feel I had more responsibility. One responsibility was to arrange for showings with the homes for sale. To arrange the showings I had to multi task, something no one let me do since the injury. The job gave me a feeling of accomplishment and an overall feeling of pride. For the first time since the injury, I was proud of the work I was doing. I decided I would study to get a real estate license. It made sense to do so because Adam was involved in real estate. I had background knowledge from the Board of Realtors and experience in a private real estate office. I found a real estate office supported licensing class through, Real Estate One. It was in the evening, after work. I was one of at least 10 other students. Each class was several hours long with one break. During breaks, the students socialized. I remember one person in particular who asked the right questions to get me to talk about the car accident and my injury. I didn't discuss the accident or the injury with non-family members until this man. I remember he befriended me and we spent a couple class breaks together. This man asked, "Aren't you happy the accident happened so you could move on with your life?" I remember becoming angry at that question and told the man, "Are you crazy? NO! I would give every penny I will ever earn in the future, if the car accident could be erased from my life." I physically pushed away from the desk where we were sitting. I don't remember seeing or speaking to him after that. I told Adam of that event; Adam suggested the man was an insurance adjuster. The man's job was to determine the validity of my attorney's statements regarding my mental and physical abilities. I passed the real estate pre-licensing class and took the state-licensing exam. I did not pass. I did well on all that didn't have to do with numbers. I was very aware of real estate law from working at the Board. But, when the questions came to how many inches were needed between sockets, what is the minimum amount of inches from the floor required for an outlet, or any measurements with math story-type problems I couldn't answer. That dream was crushed. Another career I tried that didn't work.

CHAPTER NINE

A New Point of View

I would have never guessed this turning point in my recuperation, but in retrospect this was very significant in my development.

I feel very blessed with all of the different employment opportunities available to me. I recognized many different jobs I thought I had the aptitude for. During recuperation, my mind developed differently than it did when I underwent childhood naturally. During my normal lifeline, I went to cosmetology school to become a hairdresser, which was my dream since I was in elementary school. While I was working as a hairdresser, I realized I wanted a different lifestyle than I was experiencing in a salon.

I had taken a few college classes when I was in high school. My parents urged me early in my life to get a business degree. I returned to community college to perhaps get back on the path of motivation. The first thing I tried during early recuperation was to return to the business world. When I began to think my world as a businesswoman was getting on track, I hit a wall. That is when I tried to pass the exam to become a real estate agent, but was unable to pass. I took the exam twice. I tried jobs that I was certain I was prepared for with my prior experience, the special treatment I received from the Board and the job I acquired, all by myself, the Real Estate office position of receptionist.

First, I worked at the Birmingham Athletic Club, as a secretary to the General Manager. I worked well on the phone, folding and labeling letters and envelopes. With a task such as taking reservations, I did well, probably from my Experience in scheduling showings at the real estate office.

When I was asked to perform tasks that took self-initiative or problem solving, I ignored them.I didn't understand the tasks. After working for the General Manager for about three months, she came to my office and said, "I just want you to know before you read it in the paper, I am putting an ad in for your job position. You are the nicest person to hold this position, but you are also the most incompetent person we ever had". I left the BAC as soon as I could. I found a receptionist job for a private telephone business. I hated that job. I don't think the business owner was an honest man.

I was quite good with pleasantries. I was courteous and I treated clients with respect. I had a long way to go before I understood society. Generally, people speak and act in ways that are contradictory to what they really mean. Issues like empathy, honesty, integrity, and self-pride are hidden or camouflaged in verbal and physical communication. A person may describe a lady in the store in facetious terms such as 'the fashion model over there' when in reality the person was describing a lady with old or dirty or ugly clothes.

Because of the complicating use of language, I was confused when a person, especially the owner of the business and the installers, spoke to me. I became fearful that the owner of the business was making sexual advances. And when bill collectors called, the owner told me, "Tell them I would get back with them and do not to forward any calls to me (the owner)." I worked closely with the phone installers over the phone setting appointments and speaking to customers about repairs. The installers were all pleasant to me, but I was so confused when we spoke to each other. The installers discussed their opinions of women they new, woman they saw and women they interacted with on the job.

When I heard these opinions, I heard sexual references followed by laughter or spoken in quiet tones as in a whisper and in triumphant tones and wording. I interpreted many of the interpersonal relations at that job as inappropriate.

Adam and I lived together when I had that job. I never spoke to him about the sexual inappropriateness I was experiencing. I did speak to Dr. Ianni and Adam about my opinions regarding the bill collectors. I began to have dreams that my job was to lead customers into physically painful situations.

One frequent dream was that I was a controller of a tanning booth. In the dream, my boss of the tanning booth was the business owner I worked for in the real world. When people came to the tanning booth, I had to watch them in a two way mirror, the boss called my desk and told me to slowly turn the heat up on the tanning beds until the people had 3rd degree burns. I was to watch people scream and squirm in pain during this recurrent dream.

Dr. Ianni helped me determine that this nightmare came from my belief that the telephone business owner was hurting people with crooked business practices.

After months of Psychology and many discussions I decided the best thing for me was to quit.

Another business opportunity came from Janet, a long-term girlfriend I had known since I was 15 years old. My first memory of Janet comes from after I began working at the Real Estate Board, prior to the injury, and was living at my apartment with Robin.

Janet and Robin will always be dear friends of mine. I don't remember talking to Janet during my hospitalization or after I moved back to my parent's home. Janet lived in an apartment building across the main road and within walking distance from my apartment. Janet was living with Will, who I recognized at the time as a boyfriend.

In hindsight with in knowing the kind of person Janet I should have immediately understood they were married. But at the time I realized how near our apartments were to each other I think I was unable to see beyond the moment I was in.

Janet and I had been good friends before I met Robin in school. As our high school years passed, Janet and Robin came to know each other but closeness never grew between them.

The two most essential girlfriends in my life knew each other and liked each other, but never developed a friendship.

Recently, Janet told me that she did not visit me much until I had reached a healthy point in my physical and mental status. As I have acknowledged, I do not remember much from the early times after my injury. Janet seems to feel guilty when we talk that she wasn't there for me more in the early times, I don't mind. Whether Janet was or was not a regular visitor early after the injury, that doesn't matter to me. What matters most to me is that my two favorite girlfriends have continued to be my friends.

Janet helped me as I was adjusting to normal life and socialization after my injury much the same as she did when we were teenagers. I told Janet of the problems I was having with jobs, I hated my job at the telephone sales business. I shared with Janet how I had begun doing hair at co-workers homes and that I was able to find another part-time job to supplement my income. Janet invited me to start cutting her and her friends hair for more income.

Today as I reflect, I am very confused between my natural life development and my post-injury brain recreation. Some things are so far in my past, more than 20 years ago

and memories seem foggy as what happened in similar circumstances between the pre & post injury past. I am certain of specific instances but when I review instances like this my memory is blurred. I was Janet's friend and cut her hair before the injury, I know I did it again during the recreation of my brain, but just as I said, to review back-both memories seem from the same time period.

Our friendship returned to what was lost in the few years between high school and the injury. When I became frustrated and angry that I was unable to develop my work talents to the previous level of employment, Janet was working for a mortgage company. She was working a high level job at the time. When openings became available at the mortgage company, Fireman's Fund, Janet would encourage me to apply.

I applied with a resume that listed my abilities prior to the injury. My resume looked as if I was an executive secretary. I was interviewed at Fireman's Fund with Janet's recommendation.

I was given a job position at a level 9. The levels of employment were 1- 12. I worked as a mortgage processor. I worked in a cubicle in a room of women who also worked at cubicles. We all had files and telephones. My level of recuperation when I was working at Fireman's Fund was to a

128

level that when a person saw me walk, talk, socialize, use the

phone, typewriter and take notes would think I was normal.

My difficulties were much deeper than what could be seen. I

looked normal; I acted normal until I needed details.

For many months, I was asked questions daily in therapy and

in my living arrangements, as people in my life helped me

return to normal. I was good at responding to basic questions

in normal ways.

"Hi, fine how are you?" "I don't remember where the

ladies room is, can you help me?" "What are you doing for

lunch today?" Almost as though I was a secret spy, I knew the

basic social and simple work tasks but I could not

comprehend advanced work tasks. I worked for Fireman's

Fund for a few weeks, and then I married Adam and took 2

weeks off for my honeymoon.

At this time I recently had a brain scan showing my brain function to be normal. The electrical impulses of my brain activity registered with normal activity, immediately I thought I was normal. Regardless of normal or not I guess my recent pre-injury memory was still gone. Amnesia, what dates were available in my memory file and what dates were erased? Who knows? Today I don't care to discriminate between what and when, all of those memories are beyond 20 years in my past. Those memoires have no affect on the person I am today. BUT at the time the memories were my only source of reference.

While I was on my honeymoon, my supervisor and co-workers had to cover my desk and update my mortgage files. When I returned to work after my honeymoon, my supervisor, Nora, called me into a meeting.

Nora was as nice as she could be and told me what her and my co-workers had to do while I was gone to get my files ready for the end of the year. My wedding was November 11th, I returned to work before Thanksgiving. At Fireman's Fund, each mortgage they held needed taxes paid by December 31st. I remember Nora asked me, in the weeks before my wedding, every morning and afternoon, how I was doing.

I always replied that I was doing fine. My mind understood the words Nora used and she asked how I was doing in the same way everyone says, "Hi, how are you doing?" My regular consistent response since the injury was to say, "Fine." I always told Nora I was fine. I am sure, due to the level I was working; Nora never imagined I did not understand how to perform my job. She never directly asked me if I was working on the files on my desk. I did open all my files, alphabetized the papers, and straightened them out. If something was not read- able, I retyped it. I was doing what I thought was fine.

Nora explained to me that the position I held was not right for me. I still had a job with Fireman's Fund and employment benefits, but it was in a different department. I was demoted from position 9 to position 1. I became a file maintenance person. I worked in the basement with the retards! I can't even begin to tell the emotional trauma I went through with that demotion. I was blessed by that job in that I made some new friends and I learned more about life and socialization.

I met one of my previous co-workers from the level 9 department on breaks and we discussed options that might be available to me to work in a position where I was not in the basement.

While I was working in file maintenance, I met a job coach. The job coach was an individual paid by a private company to help the mentally disabled mainstream into the normal work force. I learned and watched the job coach for weeks. When I met my friend from my previous position on breaks we looked at the want ads.

I began to circle job positions I knew nothing about and when

I was home I called on them.I called on a job posting for an
Occupational Therapist

"Hi, I am calling about the ad in the paper" "I have a few
questions, do you have some time to talk to me" "I was head
injured, lived, was in a coma for seven days, rehabbed, and
am trying to enter the work force again. Do you think, with
my medical history I would be of benefit to O.T.?"

The person on the other end talked to me for a few minutes
and asked me questions. "I certainly think you would benefit
the therapy department, maybe not as an O.T. but as a
C.O.T.A." I distinctly remember her saying.

I spoke to my break friend, the job coach, Adam, Robin
and my family about the job of C.O.T.A. I studied what that
job position entailed.

At one of my psychology sessions I discussed going back
to college for O.T. at length with Dr. Ianni. He said he could
contact my insurance company to get reimbursement for my
schooling and he would help me learn to study. I spoke to a
college counselor to find out what credits I needed to graduate
with an Associate of Applied Science Degree in O.T. The
degree was a 2-year college degree, after basic education pre-

132

requisites were completed. Prior to the injury, I was a few classes shy of my Associate's of Arts Degree in Liberal Arts. I went back to Oakland Community College to complete my Associate's Degree and prepared to attend Schoolcraft College for a C.O.T.A. degree.

I thank Fireman's Fund for opening my mind to health care. Before any O.T. classes, I began working part time at group homes. The first group home I worked for was an adult home for the head injured. I knew working with the head injured would be a test to see if I could emotionally handle seeing and helping other people who were living the life style I prayed I would not have to.For the group homes I had medication training and basic health care training. The company I worked for required caregivers to pass tests regarding privacy and mental disability When I watched slides, movies and sat through lectures about the mentally disabled, I had an awakening to the similarities of head injuries and different mental disabilities. I immediately recognized and agreed with what was taught regarding ignorance of the general public in regard to any type of mental difficulty.

I learned that many people who suffer mental difficulties also suffer from physical difficulties. Every time I saw a slide or movie that depicted actual people living with the family of and among the head injured, I was able to visualize a time in my recuperation. Especially the anger and frustration from care givers and the head injured themselves. The next group home I worked at was for the developmentally disabled. Most of the residents were born with Downs Syndrome. While working in the last group home I was in school for O.T., I met caregiver staff, administration, medical personnel, state inspectors, the residents, and their families. One of the residents was a girl, Chrissy, who was born the same year as I was: 1962. Chrissy was non-verbal. She made sounds and mostly had physical outbursts. I found a kinship with her. When I worked evenings at the group home, I spent one-on-one time with Chrissy. I hugged her and told her stories of what it was like to grow up during the years she and I did. I easily remembered everything from my past. I told Chrissy how I had a Donny Osmond poster in my bedroom, and that I listened to Bob Seger when I was a pre-teenager.I told Chrissy what it was like to graduate from high school in 1980. I told her what it was like to go to a prom and school 134 parties. I credit Chrissy with helping recognize memories of my teenage years. Adam has helped me incredibly with life happenings. When I graduated from Day Rehab, I was overjoyed with my accomplishments. I continued through college and into my professional life with encounters of happenings that were familiar to me. Some happenings were therapy related, while others were learning situations. I will never forget, after Adam and I were married and I had begun college again, I wanted to ride a bike. When I was a child, I learned to ride a bike the same way most people do. I had to put a lot more effort into learning to ride a bike as an adult. I re-learned as an adult on an old bike. The balance did not come back, it had to be re-experienced and re-learned. Once I learned, I loved it! Adam has a passive personality trait in which he can assist someone without the person knowing he had done anything. I don't remember attempting to ride a bike, the second time around, but I remember the day I independently biked down the street of the first home I lived after Adam and I were married. That following May, Adam bought me a mountain bike for my 30th birthday. I rode that bike every chance I had.

CHAPTER TEN

College

In trying to become normal and live a life be-yond the injury I
consulted with Dr. Ianni, Adam, and his Dad who had been
my community college professor prior to the injury, my
parents and friends. I made a life changing decision to go to
college so I could get a Certification as an Occupational
Therapy Assistant. I decided to a search for a local school that
was recommended by the health care community. I found
Schoolcraft College in Livonia, MI. I finished my pre-requisite
courses such as college algebra and beginning anatomy back
at Oakland Community College.

I have many memories of college, most of them pleasant, I
remember anatomy class. The class worked with cat cadavers,
our professor told us that a cat's internal organs are set up in
the same locations as humans. The students were paired up; I
had a male partner who was wishy/washy about the whole dissection thing. We were given dead cats in bags of embalming
fluid. Our first assignment was to skin them. We learned how
to separate the skin from the skeleton, once the cat had no
skin or fur we had access to the internal structure. Because of
the cat lover I am, I laid my cat on the table and covered his

136

face with a wet paper towel. The instructor went around to
each dissection table to monitor progress. The professor asked
my partner,"Why is the cat's head covered?"

"I don't know. Ask her."

I looked up as I was skinning my cat. "I love cats and the
only way I can do this is if I don't have to look it in the
eyes".The professor smiled, nodded and moved to the next
dissection table. The class was in session one night a week
and the lab was open all week for partners to complete the
assigned dissections, and to study the internal.organs. Each
week we learned about different organs, their location of and
how they worked with surrounding organs. I met my partner at
least one time outside of our regular class each week in the
evenings to study. Adam and I were already married during
the time I was taking anatomy. I became familiar with the
smell of embalming fluid and didn't think twice about any
residual scents I may have on my clothes. On several different
evenings after I returned home from anatomy class. Adam
mentioned that I had an unusual odor. I thought nothing of it.
One evening in particular, I remember Adam wanted to take
me out to dinner.

When I got home from class he gently said, "Why don't you go in the bathroom and freshen up?" I went to the bathroom, fluffed my hair, brushed my teeth, checked my lipstick and returned to the living room to meet Adam. When he moved close to me, Adam said, "Lori, are you ok? You smell like you vomited?" I forgot I smelled like the anatomy lab. "Oh sweetie, it's left over from class, let me quick change my clothes." Adam had been my guardian angel all through hospitalization, therapy, and adult re-development. I am lucky to have had him. He has always been introverted and very sensitive to the impression he gave others along with how people may view me. Adam used the same methods he learned in early on development to help me. If a situation occurred during any of my redevelopment that could tarnish my character, Adam prepared me and discussed the event with me, and then helped me problem solve.

If he took me to the mall and I was openly displaying a fear of the escalator, Adam would take my hand while he calmly whispered to me that it would be ok and he would help me. With his support, I was strong enough to try. I looked at a moving staircase and realized I required good balance and the ability to move quickly or I would fall. With Adam's hand and emotional support, I had no worry of falling.

Adam used a lot of forethought when he spoke to me. I remember speaking to Adam, my words did not come out as I wanted them to and I could not express my thoughts accurately. Adam would blink, take a deep breath, and calmly ask me to explain. When I learned I could rely on Adam, my socialization developed.

During inpatient rehab, outpatient rehab, and into my return to a normal life, Adam tried to help with all my physical and mental difficulties. Many times Adam knew he had to speak up and tell me when something was wrong, to help me be the person he knew I could be.

I am giggling to myself right now, I remember Adam's expression and the difficulty he had when he would make mention of a fashion or appearance mistake. "Lori, lets go get your eyebrow's plucked" or "Come here, let me straighten out that blouse" Today I ask for Adam's opinion on my outfits and re refuses to comment, the most I can get out of him now is if I question "Do you like this...or this better?"

Many different events happened during college I could fill an entire book. I had good and bad events happen. I met many very interesting fellow students and built a good relationship with my favorite instructor, Mrs. Milligan. She was one of my professors each semester and each year of OT classes. The first of the two years in classroom studies were very emotional for me. Those of us in the COTA program had to keep a 3-point grade average to stay in the program. Oh my God! I was previously told when I was still an inpatient that I my educational level stopped at eighth grade. I was told I would never return to college. With the support of my friends and family, I never gave up. In the fall of 1988, Adam and I were living together in an apartment. With his emotional support, I took classes at Oakland Community College to see if in fact was able to further my education. I passed the first class I took! I was beating the odds. I was able to improve more than the medical professionals originally thought possible. I with classes for the e degree I had begun back when I was working at the Board and prior to my injury. I did complete the Degree. After attempting and completing my Associates I gained confidence that I could do more. I knew I had a treacherous road ahead, but I knew I could do it.

This time, college was not a personal test to see how well I could do. I was attending college for OT because my new goal in life was to help other people. The jobs I had in group homes and spending personal time in therapy sessions taught me how important proper care was for everyone who had any kind of brain malfunction. I specialized my studies in neurology, actually the study of improving memory skills. I have known many neurology professionals since the injury and admire them for their patience, the years of study it takes, and the calm, accepting attitude they must posses to perform their job. I now privately call myself a memory specialist.

I structured my studies so that I concentrated on the thought process of humans. When COTA classes began, all the students came to befriend each other. I would say more than half the class consisted of non-traditional aged students. I was a non-traditional student, in that I was 28 when I began the program. Most of us in class had families of our own. I was the same age as many other students. I was married, but most of the other students my age were parents and most of them were divorced. I had no children, but I lived in an adult independent home and was married. As I was growing up, I recognized that I had a terrible temper. Back in my early teenage years, I Verbally fight with the best. I said thing that today I am sorry for, and I unintentionally hurt people with my temper. The temper I demonstrated was not one that I was proud of. I never tried to control my temper, my temper was a part of my pre-injury personality.

In high school, I took all the classes I could that were available regarding childbirth and development. I knew then that the most important job a person could ever have is that of a parent. Because of my terrible temper, I knew I could not be the superior person a parent should be. I decided early in my life that I would never have children.

When Adam and I became steady and faithful to each other in our dating relationship, I told him of my desire to not have children. I told Adam if he wanted children he should find a new girlfriend. Adam hugged me, "Don't worry, I just want you." I told my classmates and instructors of my physical history and the therapy I had over the years. When I was a patient of Occupational Therapy I hated it.

I couldn't see how my performance in that therapy could help me grow to live a normal life again.

Then when I was close to graduation from OT, I remembered the therapists at the hospital, at the time I lived assisted in my parents house and attended Day Rehab, asked me what gave me trouble at home and what was important to me personally. After that is when I began cooking, shopping, and housekeeping in my OT sessions.

I chose OT over the other therapies to study, with the help of Dr. Ianni. He said I was too physically weak to work in the PT department and my favorite therapy-Speech required a Master's Degree. If I wanted to help people in the same way I was helped, I should look into OT.

The COTA program was a 2-year classroom program, and a 6-month clinical learning program. That schooling was beyond any basic college courses. At 28 years of age, I felt like an old lady. I had gotten past the anger from the injury in that my very important, adult development years were stripped from me. I knew I had to make the best I could with what I had.

I had to learn to how to study all over again. I had no background for socialization. After my injury, I had no background for schooling. I never was a good student until I began community college, which was for a short period before the injury.

Before I went to college for OT, I never had good study

habits. I learned quickly that study groups were wonderful. The students in the OT program met in the library, at lunch and at each other's homes regularly to study.

Initially, I was leery to join a study group. When I joined classmates at lunch and on breaks, the time was mostly spent complaining about classes and teachers. I did not want to waist a precious minute complaining.

I had done enough of that earlier in my recuperation.

I became the unofficial study monitor. Some classmates didn't appreciate it, but when I attended study groups, I would stop the gossip and bitching. I brought the focus back to OT. When we were studying for our state exams, after we had passed our OT college courses, I think everyone in the study groups appreciated my ability to keep the group on target.

Once the first year of OT had been in full swing, the students were introduced to the OT club. The current President of the OT Club at Schoolcraft came to our classes and gave a speech telling the benefits of the club. One benefit being that the president would attend the annual Occupational Therapy Conference the coming spring. When the president asked for volunteers for the position of president

and vice president, very few students came forward.
I instantly thought "If I am gonna give this a go, I am going to
jump in." A few other students and I volunteered. Just
before the election, another volunteer and I were speaking. I
said, "I can support you but I don't want to be the president,
why don't you run for president and I will go for vice."
That other girl and I won the positions. Within a month of
appointment, the newly voted in president of the OT club
changed her major in college and dropped the position. I
became the president because that was the job of the vice
president to pick up where the president needed. My class
needed a new president. The OT club was an entire new
experience for me. Prior to the injury I had been in school clubs
but never a leader. This time I was not going to be shy! I started
a nacho lunch program to help pay for my visit to the annual
convention.
When we were in study groups and students had a hard time
with different studies, I spoke up and asked the professor
to rephrase or help us to better understand. I quickly learned to
organize not only paper work but also social activities, study
groups and to study the American

Occupational Therapy Association, AOTA, newsletters and updates. In essence I had created my own college and professional therapy.

I went to the annual Occupational Therapy Convention and attended every class I could. I went to some classes that were primarily for the OTR student, Occupational Therapist Registered a longer college term is required for this diploma. I was a COTA student and that made me professionally a subordinate to the OTR, but I wanted to learn what the COTA position was. I also knew if I got my name out and spoke up, studied and met the medical reps at the convention someone would remember my name after I graduated and started looking for a job.At the convention, I purchased 20 large AOTA sweatshirts, used my visa and paid my bill when the students purchasedthe shirts from me. When our second year began at the college I asked the instructors if I could stop in their orientation classes and introduce the OT club. When I introduced the club and when we held meetings I sold the sweatshirts I told my fellow students that I paid $12 bucks each for the sweatshirts and would accept anything above that for purchase. Students were easily giving me $25 and more for the sweatshirts. I made enough money that the following class did not have to raise any funds to attend the convention the next year.

The second year of classes was very exciting; the students in second year went to various facilities where Occupational Therapy was provided on a sort of internship. The students worked side by side with a professional COTA and learned how therapy was done beyond what we read in the classroom.For almost all of the students except me, it was a new adventure. I was so familiar with the Occupational Therapy Departments in hospitals and outpatient settings that I was less impressed.

I remember telling Adam, "Going to the hospital as a student is kind of cool; it's like being a teacher in my old elementary school".

We learned different types of settings. In our first year of OT classes, we observed settings with healthy people of different ages. Our professors told us that we first needed to understand how a healthy individual functions before we learn how to help a disabled person.

In the first year, we observed daycare for both children

and adults. In our second year, we spent many hours in the many settings where OT is provided. I personally did my clinical, internship, at Beaumont Hospital's Rehab Department and St. Joseph's mental health department. I also did a clinical at, the now defunct, Oakland County Mental Health Institution. Most of the patients were people convicted of crimes who were found guilty due to mental illness.

When I was at Oakland County Mental Health, it was very hard for me. As a student, I was assigned one client per semester to study and practice therapy with. I asked the professional C.O.T.A I worked under if, when I had to review the medical notes, could I skip the part telling what the person was convicted of? I was afraid I would not be able to help if I knew.

I received good grades during my time at that clinical, but it took a few months to understand the role OT played in these facilities.

One semester, I worked with an older woman who killed her daughter. She told me, I didn't ask and I didn't want to know.

She said it was when her daughter was a child, which she regretted. But, back then she had to do what the voices told her.

The students were with the clients in open areas and guards were placed throughout the facility. I always felt safe. I worked with this older lady cooking, while we were cooking I asked her for her tips on special ways to cook because I was such a poor cook. In hindsight, I realized that OT was used in her case to help the lady take her mind off of death and her anger at herself, to help her gain independence and safety with regular life. That is sort of what I went through.

When I got to the mental ward at St. Joe's in Pontiac, I chose a client who had AIDS. Back then the disease AIDS was not openly discussed and many people who suffered from AIDS became institutionalized for their own safety, and many of them became self destructive and attempted suicide.

The man I chose as my semester project was very nice. On the first day I worked with him, we painted some ceramics.

"Want to know why I chose you for my semester project", He looked me in the eye saying, "Yes."

I replied, "Because AIDS is such a feared disease, I understand as a medical student that I can not catch it by working side by side with you or being your friend, I personally want to get past the stigma."

I remember the man smiling and touching my hand, he said he would do whatever I needed him to do for my semester project.

OT schooling was very eye opening for me. I quickly learned that what I went through as a result of the head injury is nothing compared to what other people were to live with, and possibly for the rest of their lives. After the mental institution and the mental ward at the hospital, I was more certain than ever that I wanted to help people with thought difficulties.

When I graduated from OT and received my State Certification, the most abundant and best paying jobs were with the geriatric. I had never been able to deal with blood and that is why back in high school when all of my friends were going into business or nursing. I chose business.

I had heard that all OT's did with the elderly was change their diapers and clean them up as they eat. In OT classes we were taught that working with geriatrics was much more involved than I had heard. As a professional COTA, I would be given patients to work with after they were evaluated by an OTR. My job was to utilize the techniques I learned in class to help each client reach the physical and mental goals set by the OTR. I could do that.

I vividly remember at the end of my personal sessions in OT I told my OT I wasn't strong enough to change the sheets on my bed at my apartment. My OT gave me specific exercises to gain strength and taught me to take my time and use some short cuts while changing my sheets. I continue to this day to hate changing sheets, but I was excited the first day post injury that I changed my bed sheets all by myself!

I would work to help others in the same way!

CHAPTER ELEVEN

Who Am I Today?

In 2009 or late 2008 at the original printing: As I wrote this last chapter of my memoirs I was 46 years old. My entrance to womanhood, as my mother put it, began at the age of 10. And I had been experiencing perimenopause since I was 35. I was dealing with hot flashes, I could only wear the same p.j.'s for two nights in a row. That's if I was lucky. Thank you, Dear Lord for Prozac. With medicine, I think I am handling my mood swings pretty well. I do cry more often than I used to but, it seems ladies my age embrace tears. If I didn't color my hair I probably would be 50% gray. I am generally happy every day. I credit that to my recuperation and the opportunity to continue life after my injury. It seems easy for me to find a silver lining in everything. I have many acquaintances but few close friends. I love many people but continue to have an emotional safety wall. I miss my girlfriends from my earlier life, but we all change and grow in different directions.

Let me reiterate how much I love my husband. I

completely adore Adam and pray we have many more healthy years together. Adam's family has been very loving and I am proud to be a member of his extended family. My father-in-law is a man of the world who always has a new project and a new adventure.

I have 3 brother's in-law, each of them very different. I appreciate each for his individuality, they each have truly added a new dimension to my life. I am sure our friendships will flourish.

As I write today, my brother, Chris and his wife, Marie has become newly pregnant. When Chris and I were both beginning our lives with our spouses, we decided we would not have children.

Mom was devastated and has held on to the highchair she ate from almost 70 years ago in hope to someday feed a grandchild in it. Now the Purdy name will continue for another generation, and I will be an aunt!

April 2011 Adam and I are proud Aunt and Uncle to a niece Aryanna and a nephew Izak both from my brother Chris and sister-in-law Marie.

My parents have lived through more than their share of pain, my brother born with a club foot, with mom's throat cancer and my closed head injury, my father's has had open heart surgery and two surgeries on his neck. The Purdy's have been blessed many times, we all have recuperated from our ailments and lead normal, happy lives. I believe my folks will thrive and when the day comes for their departure they will leave kicking and screaming.

In the spring of 2007, I fell out of my four-wheeled RV, while riding on the sand dunes at Silver Lake. I was riding my own-automatic-Yamaha Breeze!!!! I didn't really hurt myself, or so I thought. Immediately, I had only hurt my pride. I was kind of sore all over and I took the rest of the day off from riding.

As time went on I started feeling increased discomfort in my shoulders and arm. By the fall of 2007, I went to my general practitioner for increased daily pain, who sent me to a sports medicine doctor. Initially. I was being treated for a pinched nerve. Later, after x-rays, the beginning of arthritis in my cervical spine, C 5, was seen.

I guess I was in denial, I thought I was too young for

arthritis and never considered that diagnosis.

Medical professional colleagues have told me that the early onset of this specific arthritis is probably a result from my head injury. I have worked with arthritic people for so many years and treated them with extra kindness, giving them as much comfort as I could because arthritis is prominent in my family.

I remember my maternal grandmother had arthritis so bad in her hands that her fingers bent at the joints in all directions. She continued to make Christmas cookies almost till her death. I often tell my patients how I used to think because of the deformity of my grandma's hands the taste of her Christmas cookies was better than any other, and that they could not be reproduced.

I have pain when I lie down. I feel pain intermittently during the day when I am performing therapy. Like the good C.O.T.A. that I am, I have completely adapted my provision of therapy treatments for the pain. Tylenol extra strength and Aspercreme are my bed partners, after Adam.

April 2011, I have been a patient of Dr. Adam Rodnick for about 2 years. Dr. is a Chiropractor and I see him 3 times a week. My arthritic pain has lessened greatly. I have

developed arthritis in other joints, all of which flare when I exert myself beyond regular, such as when I hold my new niece for an hour or I plant flowers all day long. I am certain that my regular stretches and adjustments by Dr. Adam are why I rarely feel the pain I described earlier.

My Best friends: Hubby & 2 puppies ☺

For my 40th Birthday I wanted to do something spectacular. I went skydiving, I vomited about 10 times during the jump, but loved every second. I have jumped once since and never will again, fear to break my middle aged bones.

I took saxophone lessons and purchased used sax. As I
practiced I could see the geese at the pond out back, they
seemed to think I was talking to them. They screeched and
honked in return to my playing. Solo, our dog would come
into my practice room and howl while I was playing.

I practiced enough that I could play SILENT NIGHT for
my parents, Adam, Chris and Marie one Christmas Eve. Then I
developed a painful case of carpal tunnel syndrome, which I
think arose from abuse I gave my hand being a therapist, and
put my sax away.

One of the most monumental happenings during my time
as a C.O.T.A was when I was treating a gentleman who was a
stroke victim. Ever since the beginning of my professional life I
have tried to specialize in the geriatric population that needs
to work with their cognition. The man I am referring to was
introduced to the therapy department as a tough case. He had
outbursts; he couldn't communicate and was very
independent. He refused to follow direction from the doctors
or therapists. I begged to work with him, because I saw
similarities to what I lived. My most special moment with him

Dr. Adam Rodnick adjusting me.

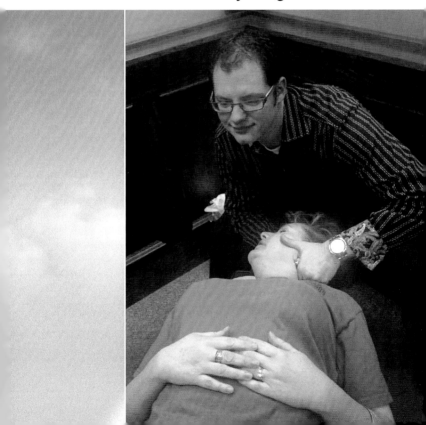

I went sky diving for my 40th Birthday!

was the day I brought my sax in. The gentleman could not blow the mouthpiece; I was concentrating on his finger movement. I put the sax in his lap and from behind him I blew while he played a riff with his fingers! I couldn't play because of the pain in my fingers and he couldn't play because of his difficulty with lungpower.

Janet and I were eating lunch the other day, we try to see each other at least a couple times a year, when she asked me, "What are you gonna do special for your 50th?" I have been thinking and have decided I want to take stand up comedian classes! Another thing I would like to do for my 50th is invite everyone I know and play all day long in Las Vegas.

In January of 2008, I hired Heather, who is a daughter of a friend, to use her composition skills as my Editor for this book. Heather has since lived through multiple brain injuries; Aneurysms, strokes and more. Heather I pray for your comfort. Since that time, I have worked diligently to complete my story. I have taken online writing classes and online workshops. I have read many books written by best selling authors, including Steven King and Janet Evanovich who gave me great inspiration, and have begun to love writing. I began writing a mystery story and I continue to have fun building it. I have a blog and I created an e-newsletter "Tomorrow is a New Day" with information I learn and articles I write to benefit brain injury survivors.

I will continue to live life to its fullest each day and try to find happiness in my every minute. I am sure my future dreams will expand on a daily basis. I am very happy being the mother of Solo, Toyo, Turbo, and Phoebe two dogs and two cats. I enjoy my life being Adam's wife. Today, my professional dreams are that of being a New York Times best selling author and a hilarious comedienne.

I realize we are all very different and our circumstances are different. I pray for everyone, we all will have our residual downfalls, I pray for everyone to have happy minutes, days, weeks, years and lives.

Yes, I AM BRAIN DAMAGED.

Lori

P.S. I am self-publishing this; again. In the original version you will remember reading a few typos and if you paid very close attention I made one name mistake. OMG! I so appreciate typesetters and printers. I have decided to stop with this the 3rd or 4th final review of this self- published copy, every time I think I have it, I must learn more. **I have added some insights as I see my world today.** I want this book or a different version to be picked up by a large publishing company who will then make this a professional piece. Most importantly I want this information out to the world. All health professionals and non-professionals could benefit from my insider's view of Traumatic Brain Injury, this is a great story with a wonderful and happy ending so this will encourage and empower all people of the non-brain injured world. And lastly I am looking to create an audio version of this book for my fellow brain injured who have difficulty reading.

FOR PERSONAL SUPPORRT I SUGGEST:
Brain Injury Association of America 1608 Spring Hill Road, Suite 110 Vienna, VA 22182
Phone: 703-761-0750   Fax: 703-761-0755
FOR MY HOME STATE: The Brain Injury Association of Michigan (BIAMI) Toll-Free Help Line: (800) 772-4323

Thank you, Thank you, Thank you, Thank you, Thank you
Thank you, Thank you, Thank you, Thank you, Thank you

With everything I have and everything I am I devote this to book to you:

The people who have loved and encouraged me 24/7 since 1986: My **HUSBAND** , My Brother Chris, My Mother Jean and My Father Ed. I have seen many other survivors and many different avenues for recuperation. Everything you did, every minute you gave to me has been a blessing. Thank you Good Lord for these angels and their participation in my life along with your guidance.

My Mother & Father-in-law, my in-law Brothers, all my Therapists, all CNA's, Doctor's, Nurses and Therapy Colleagues, teachers of regular learning and of rehabilitation, Karen, Janet, Robin and absolutely everyone who has touched my life!

Thank you, Thank you, Thank you, Thank you, Thank you
Thank you, Thank you, Thank you, Thank you, Thank you